OTHELLO

– a novel –

PAUL ILLIDGE

Creber Monde

For Diane and Graham Powis

Published by Creber Monde Entier
265 Port Union, 15-532
Toronto, ON M1C 4Z7 Canada
(416) 286-3988 1-866-631-4440 toll free
www.crebermonde.com

Distributed by Independent Publishers Group
814 North Franklin Street
Chicago, Illinois 60610 USA
(312) 337-0747 (312) 337-5985 fax
www.ipgbook.com
frontdesk@ipgbook.com

Design by Derek Chung Tiam Fook
Communications by JAG Business Services Inc.
Printed and bound in Canada by Hignell Book Printing, Winnipeg, Manitoba

Library and Archives Canada Cataloguing in Publication

Illidge, Paul
Othello / prose translation by Paul Illidge.

(The Shakespeare novels)
ISBN 0-9686347-7-X

I. Shakespeare, William, 1564-1616 Othello.
II. Title. III. Series: Illidge, Paul Shakespeare novels.

PR2878.O8I45 2006   C813'.54   C2006-901467-1

OTHELLO

Text of the First Folio 1623

Characters

Othello	*the Moor, General of the Venetian army*
Brabantio	*a Venetian senator, Desdemona's father*
Cassio	*a lieutenant, Othello's second-in-command*
Iago	*an ensign serving under Othello*
Roderigo	*a Venetian gentleman*
Duke	*of Venice*
Senators	*of Venice*
Montano	*governor of Cyprus prior to Othello*
Gentlemen	*of Cyprus*
Lodovico	*noble Venetian gentlemen, kinsmen of Desdemona*
Gratiano	
Sailor	
Jester	
Desdemona	*wife of Othello, Brabantio's daughter*
Emilia	*wife of Iago*
Bianca	*mistress of Cassio*

Servants, Attendants, Officers, Guards, Messengers, Herald, Musicians, Torchbearers

It's nearly midnight in 17th century Venice when two gentlemen emerge from the shadows and hurry along a narrow street beside the canal.

"No!" Roderigo snaps as the man he's walking with tries to slow him down. "Not after all the money I've already given you, Iago! And nothing more than *this* to show for it?"

"Listen, Roderigo. I had no more idea than you did," Iago protests.

"You told me you hated him."

"I do. Look," Iago says, trying to placate Roderigo, " I had three of the top people in the city vouch for me. They knew I deserved the position. But being the pompous war hero, he threw all this military language at my supporters and told them he had already chosen his new officer."

Roderigo stops and turns to Iago with intense interest.

"He's an expert in *military strategy*," Iago complains with brooding sarcasm. "His name's Michael Cassio. He's from Florence, and he just happens to have a beautiful wife as well. But he has about as much experience on the battlefield as the neighborhood knitting champion, and so I, who've fought in the campaigns at Rhodes, Cyprus and just about everywhere else, am relegated to being *His Moorship's* lowly assistant."

"Looking after his dirty work. Like being made hangman," Roderigo says.

"That's the way it is in the service now," Iago points out bitterly.

"Promotions are based on whether people like you and what your connections are. It has nothing to do with merit or ability, as it used to, when you just took the place of your superior when he was done." He shakes his head in exasperation. "*Now* do you see why there's no love lost between me and the Moor?" he asks Roderigo.

"If I were you I'd just quit."

"But the fact is," Iago says with a wily sneer, "I have a way to make working for him, work for me." Intrigued, Roderigo listens up. "It's so completely ingenious," Iago brags, "that if *I* were the Moor, I'd never have anyone like *me* working for him. Unlike some people who wear themselves out bowing and scraping for their masters, I can pretend to be completely devoted to my superior while at the same time looking out for myself – and my trusted friends, of course." He smiles before continuing to make sure Roderigo knows that includes him. "In other words, the only person whose benefit Iago has in mind...is Iago's. Whereby I get exactly what I want by doing everything I'm supposed to, performing all the duties and services expected of me, yet all along I'm turning things to my own advantage – and that of my associates, as I said. I will wear my heart on my sleeve," he scowls, "for dolts to gawk at as much as they want. But they will find I am not what I am..."

Roderigo nods, impressed. "Someone who can execute a scheme such as that deserves everything he can get."

With a gloating smile, Iago stops walking. He turns Roderigo in the direction of a palatial residence, the home of Brabantio, a man who wields great power with the government of Venice.

"Go and confront her father, Roderigo. Get him stirred up. Prod him and provoke him until he and his whole family are so anxious and concerned they're beside themselves."

"That's his house," Roderigo remarks, considering Iago's advice for a moment. "Why don't I wake him up and tell him?"

"Why not? Just be sure you shout like the city's on fire, like thieves are breaking into his house."

Roderigo makes up his mind and leaves Iago to cross the street, where he begins yelling at the top of his voice, "Brabantio! Brabantio!"

"Wake up, Brabantio!" Iago joins in. "Thieves, thieves, thieves! Watch out for your daughter! Look out for your money! Thieves!

Thieves!"

Soon the elderly, gray-bearded Brabantio, in a frenzy of confusion, rushes out onto his balcony fumbling with the sash of his dressing gown.

"What is going on?" he demands. "What's all this commotion about?"

"Is your family safe inside?" Roderigo asks.

"Are your doors locked?" Iago adds.

"Why? What's the matter?"

"Everything! You've been robbed!" Iago shouts. "You should be ashamed! Put some clothes on! Your heart's been broken and your soul's being torn in half! Right now an old black ram is having his way with your young, white lamb! Get up, for heaven's sake! Sound the alarm before Satan turns you into a grandfather, Brabantio!"

Brabantio strains his eyes through the darkness to see who's down below. "Are you crazy? What do you mean?"

"Don't you recognize my voice?" Roderigo speaks up.

"No, who are you?"

"Roderigo, sir!"

"Not again," Brabantio complains. "I told you to stop coming around my house. How much plainer do I need to be? My daughter is not having anything to do with you, and waking me up with your drunken mischief only makes things worse."

"But sir!" Roderigo protests in defence.

"You know I have the power to make trouble for you, Roderigo."

"Just a minute!" Roderigo sputters, looking to Iago for help.

"And what's this about a robbery? We're in Venice, not the countryside."

"For goodness sake!" Iago erupts. "You've got this all wrong. We come here to help you, and you treat us like petty criminals. I guess you want your daughter mounted by a black stallion? Your nephews to speak with neighs? Their cousins to be galloping steeds?"

"What vulgar man are you?" Brabantio demands, outraged by these insinuations.

"One who's come to tell you your daughter and the Moor are rutting away like a couple of animals."

"You villain!" Brabantio cries out.

"Maybe, but you, sir, are…" he pauses for dramatic effect, "a senator."

"You'll be sorry for this, Roderigo!" Brabantio storms.

Iago waves a flustered Roderigo to step forward and coaches him as he speaks.

"Sir, I take full responsibility for this. But if you'll let me continue, as I think you should, I can tell you a gondolier who works the canals has taken your daughter to be with the lecherous Moor. If you know this already, then I apologize for the trouble we've caused you; however, if you aren't aware of it, then you've been wrong to get mad. Since I am a respectable gentleman you know I would only have bothered you about something like this if you hadn't given permission for your daughter to give away her allegiance, her beauty, her intelligence and all her wealth to someone who's really no more than a wayfaring stranger. Decide for yourself. If she's at home in bed, then bring the state's punishment down hard on me for upsetting you like this."

Without hesitating, Brabantio turns to go back inside, calling for his household staff to awake and light the candles. Under his breath he admits that, as chance would have it, he's had a bad dream about this very thing…

Events proceeding according to plan, Iago bids Roderigo farewell, explaining that it won't look good if he appears to have been disloyal to the Moor, his master.

"I also know how the government will react," he confides to Roderigo. "The commotion it stirs up will be nothing more than a temporary setback. They need the Moor for the war in Cyprus, which is already underway, and they have nobody else as qualified to lead the campaign. So although I hate him, I have to appear to be doing my duty by him. But like I said, it's only a front. Take the search party to The Sagittarius. I'll meet you there!"

He dashes off just as Brabantio and his servants come charging into the street with lit torches flaming.

Flustered and distraught, old Brabantio fusses to do up his housecoat but he can't because his hands are shaking too much. One of his servants sees the trouble he's having and runs alongside him trying to tie his master's belt.

"It's true, she's gone," Brabantio admits gravely when he reaches Roderigo.

"What's my wretched life going to become except never-ending bitterness. Where did you see her, Roderigo? The poor thing – with the Moor, didn't you say?" Brabantio inquires frantically. "Why be a father when this is what happens to you – how did you know it was my daughter? She's deceptive beyond belief," he declares. "I can't bear to think about it. What did she say to you? Get more lights! Wake the whole family! Do you think they're married?"

"I'm afraid so, sir."

"Heaven have mercy! How did she get out? Betraying her family's trust! Fathers everywhere, don't put any faith in what your daughters tell you – they'll just turn around and do whatever they feel like. Aren't their potions and spells people can use to seduce women like this? Haven't you heard about that, Roderigo?"

"I have indeed, sir."

Brabantio babbles to himself disjointedly before turning to his household staff, many of them still getting dressed as they make their way into the street with freshly lit torches.

"Contact my brother!" he commands. "If only I'd given her to you, Roderigo. Some of you go that way, the rest come along here! Do you know where we can find her and the Moor?"

"I believe I do, sir. If your men are ready I'll take you there."

"Lead the way then. I'll knock at everyone's door as we pass – the neighbors will be obliged to help. Bring your weapons! Call out the night guards! Let's go, Roderigo – I'll make this worth your while."

Torches burning outside *The Sagittarius* shimmer on the dark water of the canal. Gondolas become visible when they pass within the torchlight and then continue on quietly through the Venice night. Whenever the door to the inn opens, the noise of people celebrating inside fills the night air briefly; tipsy patrons help each other outside and bid farewell to their friends under the red sign that hangs above the inn door: a golden centaur – a creature with the head of man and the body of a horse – rearing up on its hind legs…

Iago has brought Othello, the dark-skinned General in charge of the Venetian army, out to the street so he can report the news about Brabantio. Though he's listening, Othello is more intent on a gondolier poling his boat along the canal, his passengers a man and a woman locked in passionate embrace in the dim light of the gondola's lanterns.

"So what if I've killed men fighting them in battle," Iago rages, "cold-blooded murder goes against my conscience – that's why I've never gotten ahead like some people I know. I'm not willing to sacrifice principles just to get promoted…"

Keen to see what affect his tirade is having, he peers up at Othello The General remains lost in his own thoughts, so Iago tries a different approach. "Nine or ten times I could have stuck him right there – " he declares menacingly, stabbing the air in front of Othello repeatedly, "– right between the ribs!"

"It's just as well you didn't," Othello responds, his eyes following the gondola with the lovers as it glides silently off into the night.

"No, but the thing is, he railed on against you in the most offensive language so that even with the little bit of religion I have it was all I could do to restrain myself from shutting his mouth. So tell me, sir, are you already married? I'm sure you're aware that Brabantio is so esteemed in Venice that his voice carries double the weight of the duke's – he could demand an annulment or have the authorities come down on you with the full force of the law and no one could oppose him."

"Let him do his worst," Othello replies without concern, "the services I have rendered to the state will speak more loudly than his worst complaints. As for my marriage, it is not yet known – though when the time is right I'll make the appropriate announcement in honorable fashion – don't forget I've spent my whole life dealing with people of lofty standing. It's through them that I've managed to reach my own high position, one that requires me to take my hat off to no one. And you should know, Iago, even if I weren't in love with the gentle Desdemona, I wouldn't let my freedom to marry who I want be challenged for all the treasure buried in the sea. But look, what lights are those coming this way?"

"The livid father and his friends. You'd best go back inside."

Brabantio, with a contingent of angry-looking fellow citizens wielding swords, is moving toward *The Sagittarius*.

"Not I," says Othello. "I will let them find me. My conduct, reputation and character are well above reproof. Is it them?"

"If my eyes don't mistake me."

"Isn't that the Duke's men approaching from the square? And my lieutenant…?"

Iago turns and glances toward the nearby square where Othello's lieutenant, Michael Cassio, quick-marches an armed unit of soldiers up to the door of *The Sagittarius*.

"A pleasant good evening to you, my friends," says Othello. "You look as though you have news, Lieutenant Cassio…"

"The duke offers his sincere greetings, General, and asks me to convey his urgent request for your immediate presence at the palace."

"What is the matter?"

"Something concerning Cyprus as I gather; there's such considerable alarm that Venetian spies have sent a dozen messengers in quick succession tonight, and many of the city consuls are already assembled and awaiting you at the duke's. They've been desperate to locate you – when it was discovered you weren't at home the Senate dispatched three search parties to track you down."

"It's a good thing you found me then," Othello smiles. "Let me have a moment before I go with you." He walks to the door of *The Sagittarius* and slips inside.

Cassio sizes up the inn, the expression on his face indicating his disapproval.

"What brings the General here, Ensign?"

Iago glares at Cassio. "Why, tonight he boarded a treasure ship: if it proves to be a lawful conquest, his sailing days will be over…"

"I don't understand."

"He's married," Iago says and throws Cassio a prurient wink.

"To whom?"

"Why, to her who – " But seeing Othello returning, he breaks off. "Come, General, shall we go?"

"Lead the way," Othello replies. He moves to step past Cassio but the lieutenant holds him back with a cautioning hand.

"Seems another troop is hunting for you…"

"Brabantio, General," Iago blurts. "I'd be careful. His intentions aren't the best…"

When Brabantio's delegation is close enough, Othello hollers to them. "Attention, gentlemen. Stand your ground."

"Senator," Roderigo murmurs nervously, "it is the Moor."

But Brabantio is not to be dissuaded. "Down with him, the thief!" He takes out his sword, a cue for his citizen followers to draw theirs – which triggers Cassio and his soldiers to do the same.

"You, Roderigo!" Iago shouts menacingly. "Come sir, I'll take care of you."

Puzzled, Roderigo stops and waits a safe distance from Othello while Brabantio storms ahead.

"Keep your bright swords in their sheathes," the General warns as Brabantio continues to advance, "or the night mist will rust their fresh new metal before the fight begins. Good sir, you'll command more respect with age than with belligerence – "

"Detestable thief! Where have you stowed my daughter? Damned as you already are, it's obvious to anyone with a grain of sense that you have bewitched her – or why else would a girl so wholesome, tender and happy – so opposed to marriage she spurned the cream of Venice's bachelor crop – why else, I say, would she risk being mocked and scorned for leaving the comfort and security of her privileged position to hide in your sooty embrace? It could only be out of fear, not to seek pleasure. As the world is my witness, I say it is obvious to any sensible person that you have preyed upon her with your sinister spells and abused her delicate youth by plying her with pernicious potions: which an investigation will in all likelihood determine to be the case. Thus, I arrest you and demand you be held as a practitioner of corruption for dealing in black magic, which is expressly forbidden, as well as illegal in the state of Venice. Seize him," Brabantio says to his followers. "If he tries to resist, subdue him at his peril!"

The moment Brabantio's men move on Othello, his soldiers close ranks and prepare to defend him.

"Put down your weapons, all of you," Othello orders in a firm, deep voice. "I know when it's time to fight without anyone telling me. Where would you like me to go to answer these charges, Brabantio?"

"To jail, until such time as through due process of law a trial can be arranged."

"And let us say I obey. How would the Duke take it if the messengers he sent to retrieve me on urgent state business returned to him empty-handed?"

"It's true, senator," an officer pipes up, "the Duke's council is in session and I'm sure your eminent person has been sent for also."

"What's that?" Brabantio snaps. "The Duke in council? At this time of night? Take him away," he says sternly, waving his men to apprehend the General. "Mine is far from a frivolous case, Othello, and as a fellow senator, the Duke cannot but feel this wrong as though it were his own. Why, if culprits like you are allowed to go free, then slaves and heathen our statesmen will be."

Surrounded by attendants, with official messengers coming and going, the Venetian senators have gathered in the candle-lit Council Chamber at the Duke's palace: papers, maps and nautical charts spread out on the wide, burnished gold table in front of them.

"There is no consistency to any of these reports which makes them credible," the Duke points out.

"Indeed, they are all out of proportion," the first senator agrees. "My letter indicates 107 ships."

"Mine puts the number at 140."

"Mine suggests 200," the second senator offers, "but though they don't agree on estimates – as guesses tend to be inexact in cases like this – yet they all confirm a Turkish fleet heading for Cyprus."

"I believe there is enough to go on, despite the discrepancy," the Duke rules. "The main point, ominous though it is, I take to be true."

"What ho, what ho!" a sailor alerts those in the hall and a moment later is whisked into the chamber, accompanied by an officer who announces that the messenger is "from our spies."

"Very well. What is the latest situation?" the Duke inquires.

"The governor of Cyprus bid me tell you that the Turkish fleet is making for Rhodes."

The Duke's face registers surprise. He turns to the first senator. "Why would they have changed direction?"

"It can't be – it doesn't make sense, except as a ruse to divert our attention. Consider the significance of Cyprus for the Turks, how possessing it concerns them far more than Rhodes, especially since it can be taken so easily, having nowhere near the defensive capabilities Rhodes is prepared with. We mustn't think the Turks are so ignorant as to leave that for last which concerns them first, foregoing a smooth and painless assault for one that is sure to be risky and dangerous."

"True," the Duke agrees. "I think it's safe to say they are not heading for Rhodes after all."

The officer motions for the guards at the door to admit a newly arrived messenger.

"Worthy and esteemed sirs," he announces, rushing up to the Duke, "the Turks bound for the island of Rhodes have there met up with a second fleet – "

"I thought so," the first senator says. "How many ships are estimated?"

"As many as thirty. And now they're circling back, brazenly bearing toward Cyprus. Senator Montano, your trusted and brave servant, sends you his unstinting devotion with this report and prays you will send reinforcements."

"There is no question but that they're bound for Cyprus," the Duke concludes. He directs a question at the first senator. "Marcus Luccicos, is he not in Venice?"

The first senator shakes his head. "He's in Florence at the moment."

"It's imperative we send word to him immediately."

The first senator nods agreement, picks up his quill pen and begins writing out the order when he notices Othello, Cassio, Iago and Roderigo have come into the room behind a furious looking Brabantio.

"Valiant Othello," the Duke begins earnestly, "we must make use of your services against the Turkish forces at once – " He stops upon noticing Brabantio. " – I did not see you, welcome gentle senator, we missed your counsel and your help tonight."

"As I missed yours," Brabantio says, looking perturbed. "Your grace, please pardon me, it was neither my position nor anything to do with affairs of state that forced me out of bed, nor was it a matter of public concern that drew me here. My particular grief is of such an emotionally overwhelming nature it feeds on and consumes other sorrows yet still retains an overwhelming power of its own."

"How so? What's the matter?"

"My daughter, your grace, my daughter!"

"Dead?" the first senator asks gently.

"To me, yes: she has been wronged, taken from me and corrupted by spells and potions administered by deceiving charlatans, which a nature like hers, being neither blind, ignorant nor insensitive, could only have succumbed to through the devilish workings of black magic."

"Whoever he be that through such treacherous course of action has thus robbed her of herself, and you of her – you shall apply the strictures of law as you see fit and pronounce sentence according to your own judgment, indeed, as though this had been my own son."

"I humbly thank your Grace. Here is the man, this Moor," Brabantio says accusingly, "whom now it seems your special mandate for affairs of state has brought to this chamber."

"We are sorry for that" and other murmured apologies are heard among the gathered senators.

The Duke turns to Othello.

"What, for your part, can you tell us about this?"

"Only that it is so," Brabantio blurts out.

"Most potent, grave and revered senators," Othello begins, nodding deferentially to the various delegations around the room, "my very noble and proven good masters. That I have taken away this old man's daughter it is most true; true as well that I have married her. Only to this extent have I offended. Unskilled am I with words, and little blessed with the soft phrases of peace, for since I was a boy of seven I have spent my life on or near the battlefield, and little of this civilian world," he says, respectfully acknowledging the table full of senators, "am I able to speak about, unless it pertains to my exploits in the broils and battles of war. Therefore I shall say little about myself in defending against these charges that Brabantio has brought before you. What I will do, should you grace me with your patience, is put forth the plain and honest truth about the course of my love, my so-called drugs and charms, my conjured spells and feats of magic: all the things of which I am accused, and to which I am supposed to have resorted in winning this man's daughter."

"A maiden so shy and retiring," Brabantio erupts, "of such a modest and quiet disposition that the slightest stirring of desire made her blush! How can it be imagined that in spite of such differences in character, age, upbringing, reputation – anything you care to name – she would fall in love with someone whom she was afraid even to look at? It is the worst kind of preposterous and faulty reasoning that suggests innocence could stray so far from the dictates of discretion – the only explanation for such unnatural behavior lying in the devious wiles practiced upon her by a cunning schemer. I therefore maintain and affirm that either through potions, whose effect is to arouse the appetite for lust, or a drink concocted for the same purpose, he had his way with her."

"To 'affirm' is well and good, but it does not prove anything unless there is evidence more substantial than these implausible assertions and improbable likelihoods based on nothing more than outward appearances."

"But Othello," the first senator intervenes, "tell us if you would. Did you through devious or underhanded means, prey upon and pervert this young girl's emotions to your own purposes? Or were the feelings a product of her own free will, of talking and questioning, in the manner of true mutual relationship?"

Othello meets the eyes of the first senator. "I beg you, send to *The Sagittarius* for the lady herself and let her talk about me in the presence of her father. If you find from what she says that I am guilty, then I will demand that you not only relieve me of my trusted position, but of my life as well."

"Bring Desdemona here," the Duke orders an officer and a detachment of guards standing across from the council table.

Othello brings Iago forward. "My ensign will accompany them – he knows the place."

Iago acknowledges Othello with a nod and departs along with the officer and his guards.

"Until she arrives," Othello says, turning to address the Duke, "as truly as I would confess my sins to heaven or present my case in a court of law, I will explain before this Council how I was fortunate enough to win this fair lady's love and she mine."

"Go ahead, then."

"Her father was a good friend, often inviting me to his house where he always liked to hear the tale of my life – the battles, sieges and campaigns I had waged over the years. I gave him the story of my experiences, from as far back as my boyhood and up to the most recently occurring. I told him of misfortunes bad luck had thrown my way, of hair-raising events on land and at sea, of narrow escapes from situations of certain death, and of being taken by ruthless enemies and sold into slavery; of how, after my eventual release, I survived arduous travels hiding in mountain caves, crossing vast, empty deserts, journeying in rock valleys whose stone walls stretched thousands of feet into the sky. I proceeded as well to describe my ordeal with the Anthropophagi cannibals, men whose heads grow beneath rather than above their shoulders, who live by eating each other.

"Hearing of this, Desdemona would stop and listen intently until household affairs drew her away. But in every free moment she hurried back and with eager ears devoured the details of my discourse. After observing this for some time, I found a suitable opportunity to talk with her alone, and was grateful to receive from her an ardent wish that I tell her the full story of my life's journey, of which she had heard only bits and pieces to that point. I happily agreed to do so, often upsetting her to the point of tears when speaking of some harsh blow or other I had suffered, especially when I was a child.

"The story done, she rewarded me for my effort with a multitude of sighs, declaring it strange, so very strange, so heart-rending, so wonderfully heart-rending. She wished she had not heard of all that had happened, and yet she wished that heaven had made such a man for her. She thanked me and insisted that if I had a friend who loved her, I should merely teach him to tell my story and he would instantly win her love. Taking her at her word, I suggested that as much as she might love a man for the dangerous life he had led, the man might love her for lending so sympathetic an ear to the story he told. This is the only enchantment I have used. Here is the lady now," he says, and directs the Council's attention toward the chamber door where Desdemona has come in, accompanied by Iago, the officer, and his guards. "Let her bear witness to these words of mine…"

"I think this tale would win my daughter too," the Duke comments. "Good Brabantio, perhaps you could make the best of a bad situation here: a man fares better using broken weapons than his bare hands – "

"All I ask is that we hear my daughter speak: if she admits that she did half the wooing then let the blame fall on me for mistakenly accusing this man. Come here, gentle mistress," he says stiffly, making room for her to stand with him, but Desdemona takes her place at Othello's side. Displeased, Brabantio nonetheless carries on. "Do you perceive among this noble company where your true allegiance lies?" he demands.

"Noble father, I perceive here a divided duty. I am obliged to you for my birth and upbringing, both of which have taught me to respect you. As a daughter my duty has been to you, but here is my husband: and as much proper regard as my mother showed to you, loving you over her father, so I must claim that my own proper regard is now due the Moor, my husband."

All eyes are on Brabantio as he fights to keep his composure before the Duke and his fellow senators.

"Farewell then," he says bitterly, "I am done with you. If it please your grace, let us move on to affairs of state. I realize now that it's better by far to adopt a child than have one of your own flesh and blood. Come here, Moor."

Othello steps forward.

"I give you here with all my heart that which – though you already have it – I would like to keep from you. As for you, jewel," he says, glaring darkly at Desdemona, "my spirit rejoices that I have no other children, for your elopement would make me a tyrant who would keep them ever under lock and key, to prevent such a thing from occurring again. I am finished, my lord," he breaks off, a grim-faced old man.

"Perhaps I can offer a few words to follow up what you've said, Brabantio, which advice could be a first step in helping these lovers win your favor. When situations present no hoped for remedy, and we have seen the worst instead to happen – not what we earlier pinned our hopes upon – it's often because we see what has transpired as the worst, since it isn't what we wanted. To mourn a misfortune that is past and gone is the nearest way to bring new mischief on. When fortune takes away what cannot be from fortune's grasp protected, patience, by such loss, is unaffected. The robbed one who smiles, steals something from the thief; he robs himself who dwells on pointless grief."

"So let the Turks take Cyprus in the meanwhile – we lost it not, so long as we can smile?" Brabantio asks pointedly. "He bears strict judgment well who nothing bears except the coldest comfort of consoling words, which thereafter are all he hears. But he bears both the judgment and the sorrow who, to help his grief, must from "poor patience" borrow. These sentences, one sugar, one bitter gall, being strong on both sides, are in the end equivocal. And words are only words: I never yet did hear of a battered heart that was healed via the ear. Again, I humbly say, carry on with the affairs of state."

The Duke waits to receive affirming nods from his fellow senators then turns his attention solemnly back to the business at hand.

"The Turks with a mighty fleet are coursing toward Cyprus. Othello, the defenses of the island are best known by you, and though we have in Governor Montano a man of sound ability, still we would feel safer with you in command. You must therefore be prepared to have the luster of your newfound treasure too soon tarnished with this most difficult and formidable enterprise."

"Most revered senators, cruel custom has made sleeping on a stony battlefield like slumbering in the finest feather bed. I am no stranger to fierce challenges, so it is with cheerful eagerness that I accept responsibility for meeting the Turkish siege. If it so please you, I most humbly request arrangements be made for my wife to accompany me, with appropriate consideration for her social position in accommodation that provides the sort of company as befits one of her background."

"Why, she could stay at her father's."

"I will not have it so," Brabantio objects.

"Nor I," says Othello.

"Nor would I want to live there," Desdemona submits, the mere sight of me provoking my father's anger and resentment. Most gracious Duke, lend a favorable ear to a proposal if you would, and consider it in light of my honest asking."

"What do you have in mind, Desdemona?"

"That I did love the Moor enough to live with him in scornful disregard of all convention will soon be well known. My heart has accepted everything about my husband's life and work: I have seen past his face to the true qualities of his mind, and to his personal gifts and attributes I am devoted in body and soul, so that, dear lords, if I were to be left behind, idling peacefully at home while he goes off to war, the privilege of loving him will be taken from me, and I will be forced to endure a distressing emptiness while he is gone. Allow me to go with him," she pleads, meeting the Duke's eyes with her own.

"Grant her your approval," Othello says. "As heaven is my witness I'm not asking so that I can satisfy the cravings of desire, nor give in to unbridled youthful passions, my lust for which has long been extinguished, but to be free and generous to her mind. And heaven forbid good sirs that you would imagine by her presence I would neglect the serious mission with which you have entrusted me. No, the day that love's languor finds me lolling in the sheets instead of doing my diligent duty, will be the day that cooks make a skillet of my battle helmet and all base, unworthy adversaries rightly denounce the esteem in which I am held."

"Let the staying or going be privately determined, then," the Duke declares impatiently. "The Turkish business requires our utmost attention."

"You must leave tonight," the first senator informs Othello.

"Tonight, my lord?" Desdemona asks.

"Tonight," decrees the Duke.

"With all my heart," Othello replies, meeting Desdemona's eyes with a reassuring look.

"We will convene again at nine tomorrow morning. Othello, leave an officer behind and he can relay our formal commission to you, along with other documents that will concern you."

"If it please your grace, my ensign Iago will remain: he's a man of honesty and trust. I will leave him to escort my wife and convey whatever else your grace will need to send after me."

"Let it be so, good night all. And worthy senator," the Duke says to Brabantio, "if virtue should delighted beauty ever lack, your son-in-law is far more fair than black."

"Farewell, brave Moor. Look after Desdemona," the first senator offers.

"Watch her Moor," Brabantio says coldly, "if you have eyes to see. She has deceived her father and well may thee."

Ignoring Desdemona, he turns away from Othello and follows the Duke, his fellow senators and the other officials as they depart.

Iago comes over to stand beside Desdemona, a smitten but disgruntled Roderigo hovering behind him.

"I would stake my life upon her loyalty," Othello says defensively when the others are gone. "Honest Iago, my Desdemona I must leave with you: I pray you, let your wife assist her and follow after at the first opportunity." He takes his wife gently by the arm. "Come Desdemona. I have but an hour to spend on marriage matters and instructions for Cyprus – we must meet our obligations in this emergency promptly."

The moment they have left the Council Chamber, Roderigo steps forward.

"Iago!"

"What's wrong, my good man?" Iago replies nonchalantly.

"What should I do now?"

"Go home to bed and get some sleep."

Roderigo pauses in confusion.

"I'm going to drown myself," he declares after a moment. "The first chance I get," he adds when Iago doesn't respond.

"If you do, we won't be friends anymore," Iago says in an offhand way. He looks Roderigo in the eye. "Why would you do something like *that* you silly fellow?"

"Because it's foolish to go on living when living is such torment. We have a right to die if death is the only thing that will heal us."

"Nonsense! I've been on this earth for forty-seven years and ever since I could distinguish between what's helpful and what's hurtful I've never met anyone who knew how to love himself. If the love of a cunning harlot was the reason I wanted to drown myself I'd just as soon change places with a baboon."

"Well what should I do? I admit it's shameful to be as infatuated as I am, but I haven't the power to control how I feel."

"Power? Rubbish," Iago sneers, leading him into the hall. "It's completely within our power to control who and what we are," he says as they walk, Roderigo hurrying to keep up. The body is a garden in which the will is gardener. So, the decision to plant nettles or sow lettuce, plant hyssop or grow thyme, start one kind of herb or several – to let the soil lie fallow or fertilize with manure – why, the whole thing boils down to our own willpower. If we didn't have reason to keep our raging emotions in check, our animal nature would simply turn us into perverse monsters. But fortunately we have reason to control our worst impulses, our carnal cravings, our urges and desires, which is why what you call love, I take to be a mere flower-cutting the garden can easily live without."

"It can't be – "

"It can and it is – merely an excitement of the blood your will allows you to feel. Come, be a man! Drown yourself? Drown cats and newborn puppies. I have always called you my friend, Roderigo, and I confess I'm tied to your success in this venture with the strongest cord. I've never been able to help you more than I can now. Raise yourself some more money, head to Cyprus and observe the fighting, disguise yourself with a distinguished-looking false beard. I tell you, raise more money, Roderigo. Desdemona's love for Othello won't last long – mark my words – nor his for her either. She rushed headlong into it and you will see it end just as suddenly – so make sure you have your money ready." He starts down the palace stairs, Roderigo.struggling to keep pace with him. "These Moors are known for changing their minds – fill your wallet with money. I promise you this: food that at the moment is as luscious as leaves to locusts will shortly be as bitter as a crab apple. Besides, she needs a younger man; when she's had her fill of his body she will see the error of her ways: she must have more, she must. Therefore, as I say, get all the money together you can. If you want to go to hell by killing yourself, at least do it in a more stylish way than drowning – hunt down every dollar and ducat you can. A sham religious ceremony and a frail vow between a randy Barbarian and a crafty Venetian vixen are not likely to get the better of me – I say you will have her Roderigo! But make sure you're ready with the money. Forget drowning yourself; it's going about things the wrong way. Better to go down with the ship and her wrapped in your arms than throw yourself overboard without her."

They come outside into the dark street.

"Can I count on you to be with me in this?"

"You can depend on me completely – go, raise your money. If I've told you once, I've told you a hundred times: I hate the Moor. My cause is as heartfelt as yours: we're bound together by our desire for revenge. If you can sleep with his wife and make him a cuckold, you get your pleasure and I my amusement. The future has much in store for us, Roderigo. So get going, round up the money: we'll talk more about this tomorrow. Adieu!"

"Wait!" Roderigo calls and runs after the departing Iago. "Where shall we meet?"

"At my house."

"I'll be there first thing."

"Good, now farewell – and remember what I told you."

"What's that?"

"No more talk of drowning, all right?"

Roderigo nods. "I've changed my mind anyway. I'm selling my property."

Iago hugs him in a farewell embrace and gets on his way, glancing back a moment later to watch Roderigo stepping aboard a gondola that has stopped to pick him up. He waves goodbye as the gondola moves off along the canal.

"Farewell then," Iago says. "Just be sure you raise the money. Nothing like a fool to help line one's own pockets," he snickers and resumes walking. It's the middle of the night. The Venetian streets are quiet and deserted. "Though it *is* demeaning for someone with my talent to waste time on such a nincompoop – except that in the end it's harmless fun and reasonably profitable. The Moor is the one I hate, and it's generally thought he's done marital duty between my sheets – I don't know if it's actually true but strong suspicion in that kind of thing is as good as a guarantee. He holds me in the highest regard, which perfectly suits what I have in mind for him. Cassio's a good enough man, but let's see now…to take his place and thereby provoke double trouble would be a pretty feather in my cap. But how? How? Let's see…"

He turns and heads toward a narrow street that leads away from the water, but changes his mind and comes back. He pauses at the foot of the Ponte Vecchio, one of the many covered bridges that cross Venice's canals.

"I'll give it some time, then trick Othello into thinking Cassio's becoming overly friendly with his new wife. The lieutenant's striking appearance and alluring personality are designed to make women unfaithful. The Moor being gullible, of a free and accepting nature, thinks a man honest if he seems so and thus can be led by the nose like an ass…" He starts out across the bridge but stops suddenly. "That's it – a plan of perfect conception!" he says in triumph. "Hell and the night will engender one monstrous deception…."

Howling winds batter the rocky coast of Cyprus, a deluge of gusting rain pelting the island fortress where Governor Montano stands near the watchtower on the upper ramparts peering anxiously out to sea. Pulling his rain-drenched cloak tighter around his shoulders, he notices two gentlemen making their way along the roof platform, leaning against the driving wind.

"What could you make out from the point?" Montano shouts over the sound of the storm.

"Not a thing!" the first gentleman shouts back. "The sea is much too rough: between the port and the ocean main there wasn't a sail to be seen."

"I've never known the wind to blow like this – to shake the fortress with such ferocity: if the sea is as viciously cruel no ship's timbers will be able to withstand the mountains of water pounding her seams. What's the latest report?"

"The Turkish fleet appears to have been dispersed by the tempest," the second gentleman tells Governor Montano, " – and no wonder. Along the shore the surf hurls itself with such fury at the rocks the spray soars upward as if returning to the sky – I've never witnessed such tumult!"

Montano nods gravely. "If it happens that the Turkish ships have not taken refuge in some sheltering bay it is likely they will have gone down. It would be impossible to hold out against this – "

A third gentleman rushes up to join Montano and the others.

"Most good news, the war is over!" he announces. "The vehement storm has inflicted such damage upon the Turkish vessels that their attack has been called off. A great Venetian ship caught sight of them foundering in wrack and ruin."

"Indeed? Is this true?" Montano asks, astonished by the news.

"Quite true, sir. The ship has just put in. Michael Cassio, lieutenant to the warrior Othello, has just come ashore. The Moor himself is still at sea but is heading here with full authority to defend the island."

"I'm pleased to hear that – he's the ideal man for such a task."

"But this Officer Cassio, though he's greatly relieved by the Turkish loss, is anxious for news that the Moor is safe, for they were separated at the height of the storm."

Unbeknownst to them, Cassio has come up behind in time to overhear their conversation.

"We should pray that he is safe as well, for I have served under him and I can tell you he is an outstanding commander. Let's head to the seaside so we may meet the vessel that's come in and search the horizon between wave and cloud for some sign of brave Othello."

"Let's do so, yes, for more arrivals are expected every minute – "

At which point Michael Cassio speaks up. "Thanks, valiant warriors of this island fortress, for commending so the Moor. Oh let the heavens protect him against the elements for I lost sight of him during the worst of the tempest."

"Is his vessel good and seaworthy?" asks Montano.

"His bark is firmly timbered and his pilot a naval man of vast experience, therefore I remain optimistic that he can make it through alive."

Now that the storm has passed the rain and wind are beginning to subside.

"A sail! A sail! A sail!!" voices suddenly begin calling from somewhere close by.

"Whose voices are these?" Cassio wonders.

The second gentleman shrugs as he explains that the town is virtually deserted – but then he notices something on the brow of a hill to their right, which overlooks the sea. "The gathering crowd must have caught sight of a ship."

"Let's hope it's the new governor," Cassio offers.

A cannon shot booms across the bay.

"A courtesy shot, the friendly passage signal," says the second gentleman hopefully.

"I pray you, sir," Cassio says, "go on ahead and find out for us who is arriving."

"I shall."

"But good lieutenant," Montano asks. "Does our General come with a wife in tow or not?" He and Cassio are outside the fort now, walking toward the harbor.

"He does have that good fortune, yes," Cassio says. "Indeed she is a young woman who surpasses description, even in the most exaggerated reports. Truly, to give the quality of her nature in both body and soul exceeds the talent of our most artful wordsmiths, and in fact the task proves exhausting to anyone who tries to do her justice. Well?" he queries the second gentleman upon his return. "Who has just put in, sir?"

"Iago, ensign to the General."

"He's made excellent speed under the circumstances," Cassio remarks and glances out to sea, smiling over some private thought. "Tempests themselves, high seas and howling winds," he says, waxing poetic, "sharp rocks and sandy shallows – all the unsuspecting keel's underwater foes have doubtless sensed passing beauty and forgotten their deadly nature in order that the divine Desdemona could go by unharmed."

"Desdemona?" Montano inquires.

"The one I was talking about a moment ago, our great Captain's captain. She was put in the safe-keeping of the reliable Iago, who has managed to arrive a week earlier than we were expecting him." Cassio casts his worried gaze seaward. "Great spirit in heaven," he says, praying out loud, "guard Othello and fill his sail with your powerful breath so we may soon be favored with the appearance of his tall ship – so that Desdemona's loving arms might hold him before long. Rekindle the fire in our all but extinguished spirits and bring comfort throughout this island of Cyprus – "

He breaks off when he sees Desdemona proceeding up the path from the seaside pier with Iago, Roderigo, and Iago's wife, Emilia, who is serving as Desdemona's attendant. There is a great deal of activity as sailors, soldiers and dock hands work to unload the tall ships.

"Behold!" Cassio announces exuberantly, "the ship's richest treasure has come ashore! You men of Cyprus, let her see you on your knees!"

Iago looks on inscrutably as every man in the vicinity bows to Desdemona, making way for her to pass. Roderigo, his youthful face disguised under a false mustache and beard, goes weak at the knees when Desdemona offers him a blithe smile.

"Hail to thee, lady," Cassio says, continuing his gracious welcome by taking her hand and kissing it with almost romantic formality. "And the grace of heaven go before and behind thee, all hands encircling thee with loving care…"

"I thank you, valiant Cassio," Desdemona says in acknowledgement of his effusive treatment. "What news do you have of my lord?"

"He has not arrived yet, but I'm led to believe he's well and will shortly be here."

Desdemona glances at him uncertainly. "But weren't you and he…how did the two of you become parted?"

Cassio gestures at the gray storm clouds scudding overhead. "The great strife between the sea and the sky drove our ships apart, m'am,"

Someone close by begins shouting "A sail! A sail! Everyone look – a sail!" and a moment later a cannon thunders, firing once.

"A friendly ship greeting the Citadel," the second gentleman explains.

"Go and find out who it is," Cassio orders and the gentleman hurries off. "Welcome to Cyprus, Ensign," he says, but before Iago can reply Cassio takes Emilia's hand and presses it to his lips. "Welcome, madam." He throws a good-natured glance at Iago. "Forgive my eagerness to observe the proper courtesies – it's my upbringing. I can't help myself!"

Iago smiles ambiguously as Cassio fawns over Emilia. "Sir," he speaks up, "if only she gave as much with her lips as she does with the tongue she loves to use on me, I think you'd feel differently."

Desdemona turns to Emilia expecting a defensive riposte, but Iago's wife keeps her silence.

"You've left her speechless," Desdemona comments.

"Good God, that'll be the day. She always does this, especially when I'm trying to sleep. I swear – indeed I should point out to your ladyship – she tucks her tongue in for the night but goes on scolding with her thoughts."

"You have no reason to say that," Emilia protests.

"Come on, come on," Iago teases, "you women are prim respectability in public, nattering gossips in private, wild she-dogs guarding your territory, weepy martyrs when you feel hard done by, vindictive demons if you've been slighted – all told, you play the good wife by day, but hopping into bed…what more need be said?" Iago smiles, showing Desdemona and Emilia a suggestive wink.

"Shame on you for spouting such slander," Desdemona scolds.

"No, it's true," Iago insists and crosses himself in mock piety, "or call me a faithless Turk. You get up to play, and go to bed to work – "

"You won't be writing *my* praise any time soon," Emilia says sharply.

"No, I won't," Iago says with a sarcastic sigh.

"What would you write in praise of one like me?" Desdemona inquires.

"Dear lady, please don't press me to do that, for I'm not someone who minces words – "

"Go on, just a try," she says, " – but has someone gone back to the harbor for our things?"

"Yes, madam," Iago nods.

"Very well, so let us carry on," Desdemona decides and continues walking along beside Iago, Emilia and Cassio a step behind, Roderigo pulling up the rear.

"Suppose that I am not playful, but I disguise what I *am* by seeming otherwise. How then would you describe me?"

Iago narrows his eyes as though giving the matter utmost concentration. He holds up a hand and puts a finger to his temple. "Let me think…I'm thinking, but you see," he says, gesturing with his free hand to buy some time, "sometimes the creative essence is hard to get out – like pine-gum from hair perhaps – it brings everything else in my brain along with it. But I keep my inspired muse laboring, laboring…so that," he says, raising his index finger to signal success, "…she thus delivers the following creation: *If she be fair and wise, has fairness as* well as wit, the one will be for using, while the other uses it!"

"Very good," Desdemona smiles. "But what if she be dark and witty?"

"If she is dark and witty besides, she'll find a fair man who her darkness abides," Iago replies quickly.

"This is going from bad to worse," Desdemona complains playfully.

"What if she's fair and foolish?" Emilia asks.

Iago responds without hesitating. *"Never yet was a woman both foolish and fair, for how else but through folly does a woman produce an heir?"*

"These are trifling rhymes to make fools laugh in the tavern. What mean praise would you have for a woman who is drab and foolish?"

"There's none so drab and foolish a frump, but likes, as fair and wise ones do, the fondling of her –" He smirks and mouths the word "rump."

"How utterly unfair," Desdemona says with a mock-pouting face, "you saved your best praise for the worst! Now, if you did have to be serious, what praise would you bestow on a truly deserving woman? One who, being sure of her place in the opinion of others, fears nothing that could be said against her?"

Clearly a challenge, Iago purses his lips reflectively for a brief moment.

"She who was always fair and never proud, who was never lost for words yet never loud; she who never lacked for money yet never flaunted it, who never took what she desired until certain she wanted it; she who, being angered, kept the vengeful urge at bay, and if she felt displeasure would never say; she who in wisdom never let the pursuit of pleasure, tempt her to surrender her woman's treasure; she who knew how to think without telling what was on her mind, knew that many suitors followed, but never bothered to look behind; she who was a creature if ever such creatures were able –" Stuck for a suitable rhyme, Iago has to pause.

"To do what?" Desdemona demands.

" – to suffer fools gladly," Iago blurts, *"find the trivial...tolerable."*

"A limp and lackluster conclusion, Iago! Don't take any more advice from him, Emilia, even though he is your husband. What do you say Cassio, is he not a very coarse and flippant adviser?"

"He gets directly to the point, madam, something soldiers do better than scholars," Cassio explains, taking Desdemona by the hand and guiding her around several mud puddles.

Feeling ridiculed, Iago hobbles to the side of the path and kneels down, attending to something in his shoe, while Cassio leads Desdemona on ahead. "He takes her by the hand, yes, well done," Iago simmers, "with as slight a web as this I will ensnare as great a fly as Cassio. Yes, smile at her all you like: I will see you tangled in your own elegant manners."

Farther along the path now, Cassio gestures with his hands as he chats with Desdemona, touching two fingers to his lips when he laughs.

"You say 'That is *so* true, *so* true indeed,'" Iago sneers bitterly at the dialogue he assumes Cassio is having with Desdemona. "If these foppish flicks of the hand end up stripping you of your lieutenancy, it's only because you completely overdo things trying to be the perfect gentleman. Ah, that's good, yes, nicely done kissing her hand like that again. And what a divine curtsy, yes indeed! Fingers to your lips again! Let her see how good they are for sucking – "

A cheer goes up and trumpets sound a fanfare back at the harbor.

"The Moor!" Iago cries. "I know his trumpets!"

"It's true," Cassio tells Desdemona as she turns, a look of lively anticipation on her face.

"Let us head back and greet him."

"There is no need, madam, for look – here he comes!"

Breaking away from his troops, Othello runs to Desdemona and sweeps her up in his arms.

"My sweet warrior!"

"My dear Othello!"

They embrace each other tenderly, Othello then standing back to regard his wife, their mutual love apparent to everyone present.

"Seeing you here before my very eyes is more wonderful than I can describe! My heart's content – if every storm brings such tranquility and calm in its wake, may the winds blow till they have roused death from his bed: let my storm-tossed ship climb seas as high as Olympus before diving to the very boundaries of hell. If I were to die now I would be happy, for I know my heart has found a peace so complete that Fate can have nothing more wonderful in store for me."

"May heaven ensure that love and contentment grow more bountiful between us every day," Desdemona responds with tears in her eyes.

"By heaven's power, amen to that! I am overcome with happiness –" He puts a hand to his chest, just below his throat. "Joy chokes me up as well, my love. May this, and this," he says, kissing away her tears, "be the sole discordant note our hearts will ever have to make."

"Othello," Desdemona says softly as they embrace once more and kiss each other lovingly and long.

Over to one side Iago mutters snidely to himself: "O, you are perfectly tuned for the music I will have you make together, but being the good fellow I am, I'll loosen the strings, at least for now…"

"Come," Othello announces, "let us move to the castle." Keeping Desdemona at his side, he starts walking. "The good news, friends, is that our war is done, the Turkish fleet has foundered in the storm. How are my old comrades here on the island?" he asks, recognizing familiar faces lining the road ahead. "Sweetheart, you will be much sought after in Cyprus, for I have been fortunate in finding friendship among its people over the years. My goodness, listen to me prattling on quite out of character – dwelling so on my own personal joy." He stops and turns to look around, spotting Iago with his head bowed as he makes a pretense of listening to Roderigo's frantic chatter. "Ensign! Would you be good enough to go back to the waterfront and see that my baggage is unloaded. And bring the ship's captain up to the Citadel. He's a worthy fellow and deserves to be treated with suitable respect. Come Desdemona," he says and resumes walking, holding her close to him. "Forgive my repeating, but it is such joy to have you here with me…"

Roderigo follows Iago to a place beside the road where they can wait until the lengthy procession of soldiers, attendants and servants has filed past.

"You, and you!" Iago calls, and pulls two burly soldiers from the passing ranks. "Meet me shortly at the harbor." They salute and march promptly back the way they came. "Over here, Roderigo" he says, moving to a nearby grove of trees.

None too happy, Roderigo takes a last look at the departing Desdemona and trudges over to stand with Iago.

"If you have some courage you can muster," he begins, murmuring under his breath a moment later while Roderigo digs a stone out of his fancy shoe " – even if it's nothing more than the desperation they say weak men acquire when in love – listen up. Lieutenant Cassio is in charge of the duty guard tonight. You realize Desdemona is hopelessly in love with him, do you not?"

"With Cassio? That's impossible."

"Sst!" Iago hisses abruptly and puts a finger to his lips since a few military people and stragglers are still passing by. "Just listen, and listen carefully. Notice what a frenzy she was in when she first fell for the Moor – only because he bragged of his spectacular though much exaggerated heroics. How can she go on loving him when all he does now is chatter about how much she means to him. Well, I've got news for you: she won't. Mark my words, Roderigo. Desire like hers can only be gratified by someone considerably more appealing than a black devil like the Moor. When she's had enough of his love-making and grows bored, she will in short order need to have her inner passion aroused again, by a man who can satisfy her vigorous appetite, more handsome in appearance, closer to her own age, her way of life and her social position, than the deficient Moor. Craving these necessities for herself, her hungering youthfulness will feel cheated. She will grow sick of the Moor and find him so repulsive she will abhor him – her natural instincts compounding her anathema so she will be compelled to choose a new lover. Now, sir, given that this is so – and it most obviously and certainly *is* – who is more eminently positioned, not to say qualified, to take full advantage of this golden opportunity, but Cassio, a smooth-talking scoundrel who has no conscience when it comes to putting on the appearance of good breeding and impeccable manners to help him achieve his own lecherous ends and satiate his own most secret, immoral desires? No one, I say, no one! A cunning and slippery rogue he is, one who sniffs out opportunities with a keen and watchful eye and can turn any situation to his perfect advantage like *that*," Iago says and snaps his thumb hard, "though of course it's all contrived to make him seem something that he's not – such a devious knave is this Michael Cassio, I tell you. The plain facts are that he's handsome and young and possesses every attribute that captivates naïve young females: a deceptively poisonous character in whom our woman has found precisely what she longs for, Roderigo…"

"I can't believe that of her," Roderigo says with a pained look on his face, "she is so blessedly good in nature."

"Blessedly good, my eye! The wine she drinks is made from grapes like yours and mine. If she were 'blessedly good' as you believe, she would never have taken up with the Moor. 'Blessedly good' – rubbish! Didn't you see how she moved all over him with her hands? Did you not perceive that Roderigo?"

"I did, but surely it was relief that he had arrived safely."

"It was carnal desire as plain as this hand in front of me: the telltale prologue to a history of lust and debauchery between them. They kissed so hard their tongues could have changed mouths. There is dirty business afoot, Roderigo; when intimacies like this lead the way, hard at hand comes the main action, bodies smacking hot and hungry, panting for one conclusion. Pish!" Iago sneers distastefully. "Thus, sir, you must do what I say. This is why I have brought you from Venice. I want you to be on watch with the guards tonight. I'll arrange for you to be assigned some duties, then let you go from there. Cassio doesn't know who you are, and I'll be close by at all times. You need only do something to make Cassio angry, either by berating him or questioning his ability as a soldier, or whatever may come to mind at the time – "

"Very well," Roderigo agrees uneasily.

"Remember, he's impulsive and quick to anger – hopefully he'll strike you with his officer's staff: provoke him until he does so, for I can use the commotion to cause the people of Cyprus to riot in objection. Their attitude toward the army will remain hostile until Cassio is removed from his command. This will provide you with a short cut in getting what you came for, which I will make that much easier for you by removing this most formidable obstacle, thus fulfilling your utmost expectation of success."

"I will do this," Roderigo says again, "if you can promise me it will work."

Iago makes the sign of the cross over his heart. "It cannot fail. Meet me shortly at the Citadel. I must go to the waterfront first and bring his luggage ashore. Farewell." He waves Roderigo off dismissively then turns and heads back along the harbor road.

"Adieu!" Roderigo calls, but Iago is busy talking to himself and doesn't reply. Roderigo sighs and realizes his fake moustache is slipping on one side. He presses it back into place and starts walking toward the Citadel, limping because he still has a stone in one of his shoes.

Iago steps up his pace when the masts of a dozen tall ships in the harbor come into view. "...That Cassio loves her I am convinced. That she loves him is very likely, and perfectly credible if true. The Moor, however much I cannot endure him, is of a faithful, loving and noble nature, and I could see him as a dear, devoted husband to Desdemona. But now I want her too, not in pure and simple lust – though I could stand accused of that, it's true – but rather in my hunger for revenge, since I suspect the lecherous Moor has slipped between the sheets and topped my wife, the thought of which, like acid, burns me up inside... And nothing can or will content my soul until I even up with him, wife for wife... Or failing that, at least put the Moor into a jealousy so extreme that neither reason nor good judgment will be the cure; which I intend full well to do if this poor wretch Roderigo, whom I have reined in for so long, can rise to the occasion and let me catch the great Michael Cassio at a disadvantage, showing him in slanderous light to the Moor as nothing but a lascivious cad who preys on other men's wives." Iago stops and laughs out loud: "The Moor and I chasing him away together in our night caps!"

Arriving at the harbor, Iago spots and whistles for the two soldiers who are going to carry Othello's trunks.

"This done to Cassio, I will of course win the Moor's gratitude and affection, so he will want to reward me for keeping him from becoming a laughing-stock, even as I work upon his peace of mind and drive him into madness. It's all up here," he boasts, tapping a finger to his temple just as the soldiers present themselves. Smiling, Iago points them toward Othello's ship and follows along behind. "One or two things remain confused," he says to himself and shrugs, "but treachery's plain face is never seen until used...."

2.2

Late in the afternoon a herald from the Venetian army enters the public square escorted by soldiers and officials from Cyprus's governing council. Trumpets sound and the crowd gathers in front of the raised platform where the herald delivers a proclamation from Othello.

"It is our noble and valiant General's wish that, the Turkish fleet having gone down at sea, citizens of Cyprus should join him in celebration of this triumph through feasting, dancing, the lighting of victory fires, and citizens conducting festivities of their own choosing. Besides this joyous good news, Othello wishes to announce the celebration of his marriage and proclaims that from this present hour of five until the hour of eleven tonight, establishments are permitted to remain open and there is full liberty for one and all. Heaven bless the island of Cyprus and our noble General Othello!"

2.3

Torches are burning bright in the corridors of the Cyprus governor's castle. Othello, Desdemona and their entourage, emerge from the grand reception hall, the General bidding his dinner guests, government officials and military staff a gracious 'good night' before he leads Desdemona toward the wide marble staircase in the castle's main rotunda. She accepts a kiss on the cheek from her husband, smiles at the words he whispers in her ear, then has her attendants begin gathering up the long flowing train of her white satin wedding dress while Othello steps over to an alcove near the window for a word with Lieutenant Cassio.

"Good Michael, I think it's wise to be on your guard tonight. Let's show that we can keep our reveling within the bounds of discretion."

"Yes, sir. Iago has instructions on what to do, but I will keep an eye out just the same."

"Very good. I know we can rely on him."

Cassio stays by the window, gazing at the beautiful Desdemona, while Othello makes his way back to the stairs.

"Promises made and kept," he says joining her, "enjoyment can now ensue: the pleasure and reward for love between me and you."

Nervous but excited, Desdemona meets Othello's eyes, smiling gratefully when he offers his arm a moment before taking the first stair...

"Ah, welcome Iago," Cassio says lightly, noticing that the ensign, leaning against a wall across the rotunda, has been watching Desdemona as well. "Getting ready for duty?" he teases. Iago smiles, hoists the pewter wine cup he's holding, and takes a drink.

"It's early, lieutenant, Not even ten o'clock. The General only dismissed us because of Desdemona – although who can blame him? He has yet to spend the night with her," he says, taking another sip of wine, "'and she a prize worthy of the Gods,' as the poet once said."

Cassio nods. "She's a most exquisite lady."

"I'll bet she prefers a hot tussle over a good night's sleep," Iago winks suggestively.

"Indeed, she's a lively and vivacious creature."

"She certainly has an eye for the men! Like she's willing to *honor* any reasonable..." He searches for the right word. "*Off-her?*" he puns with a wry grin.

"Yes, her looks are most enticing, but she maintains a proper sense of modesty."

"And when she speaks. Tell me you aren't drawn to her."

"She has about her a kind of perfection."

"Well, here's to happy times beneath the sheets!" Iago toasts, but he has no wine left in his cup. "Come, lieutenant," he says, throwing an arm over Cassio's shoulder and walking him along, "I have a good bottle yonder, and as luck would have it there are several fine gentlemen of Cyprus there too. They would like nothing better than to toast the health of black Othello."

"Not tonight, good Iago. I'm not very good when it comes to drinking. I've often wished they would invent some other social custom."

"Come now. These are our friends. But one cup – I'll keep up with them after that."

"I've already had one cup tonight, carefully diluted too, yet look at the effects." He slips out from under Iago's arm, raises one foot off the ground and tries to balance on the other but can't. Iago catches him. "You see? It's an unfortunate malady I'm afraid, but I can't tax my weakness by having any more to drink."

"For goodness sake, man," Iago persists, "it's a night for celebrating – these good men deserve it."

"Where are they?"

"Here at the door. Just go and call them in."

Cassio takes stock of the situation.

"One," Iago reminds him. "Just one." He crosses his heart and holds his right hand in the air as if promising under oath.

"Very well," says Cassio, "but I'm not comfortable with it."

Iago frowns sympathetically, as though he understands Cassio's reservations.

"Where are they?"

"Here at the door. Go and call them in." Iago watches Cassio leave, running his finger around the rim of his empty cup while he reflects on matters. "I need only get one cup into him and together with what he's already had tonight he'll be as ready to bark and bite as an angry terrier. Of course my lovesick fool Roderigo, whose infatuation has turned him inside out, has drunk a full bottle in repeated toasts to Desdemona's health, so he will have to be watched. As will the three men from Cyprus, who are proud, hot-tempered types – like most on this war-torn island – since I got them well on their way to drunkenness earlier, refilling their cups well before they were drained. Amongst this flock of drunkards then, I should have no trouble prompting Cassio to something that will insult the island's people. – Here they come…if what I've planned to happen comes to be, I sail with the favoring wind on an open sea."

"Good Lord, they've had me down a full cup already!" Cassio shouts and stops Montano from pouring more wine from a bottle he's carrying while the three gentlemen from Cyprus do some hearty back-slapping.

"Just a small one," Montano protests, "barely a pint – or I'm no soldier."

Iago wastes no time leading the party along a corridor, under a covered archway and outside to a torch-lit courtyard where the dark, wooden tables, each with burning candles and several bottles of wine, are arranged around a fountain in the center: several streams of water gushing from a stone sculpture of Neptune holding high his trident.

"Some wine!" Iago calls and, taking a bottle from the nearest table, quickly fills all the cups, including Cassio's. *"And let me the wine cups clink!"* he starts to sing, motioning for the others to pull up stools. As he sings he proceeds to *clink!* each man's cup with his own. *"And you three your wine cups clink!"* he continues merrily. *"A soldier's a man, his life's but a span, why then, let a brave soldier drink!* More wine, boys!"

"By God, an excellent song!" Cassio shouts jovially, letting Iago pour him some more wine.

"I learned it in England where they drink the most potent potations. Your Dane, your German and your jelly-bellied Hollander – drink up! – are nothing compared to your English."

Slightly drunk now, Cassio's speech is slurred and he's having trouble with longer words. "Is your Englishman so ex-*quist* in his drink – so ex-*quisint* – so – " He gives up on the word and takes a breath. "In's drinking?" he asks.

"Why, he easily surpasses your Dane, who's dead drunk in no time. He out-drinks your German with no sweat at all, and he watches your Hollander bend vomiting over the bowl, even as he starts pouring the next round."

"To the health of our General!" Cassio roars and then takes a gulp of his wine.

"Here here!" Montano joins in, "I'll match that, lieutenant…and go you one better!"

"O sweet England!" Iago cheers them on and begins singing again. *"Old King Stephen was a worthy peer; his new coat bought, ten dollars was the fee. The king told the tailor his price was much too dear; paid out gold coins – not ten, not five, but three! Stephen was held in high renown, where you are but,"* he looks right at Cassio, *"of low degree. 'Tis pride that pulls your gentleman down, so keep thy old coat, as long as it can warm thee."*

"By God," Cassio shouts, this is a more ex-*quissis* song than the other!"

"Will you hear it again?" Iago calls.

"No," Cassio grumbles, his eyes drooping shut, chin upon his chest. "I consider him to be…unworthy of his position who does…such things," he mutters vaguely. "Well, but then God looks down upon us all, and there are some souls who will be going to heaven at the end, and some souls who will not."

"Very true, lieutenant," Iago tells him, a slight sarcasm in his voice.

"As for me, no offence to the General or those higher up, I hope to go to heaven."

"And so do I, lieutenant, and so – "

"Of course you do!" Cassio snaps and sits up straight, "but remember yourself, it won't be ahead of me. The lieutenant goes first, the ensign comes behind – " He sees Montano and the other gentlemen filling their long-stem pipes with tobacco. "So let us forget this and get back to business," he growls, " – God forgive us our trespassers! Gentlemen, I say, let's attend to business." Chuckling, the others continue preparing their pipes. "And gentlemen," Cassio announces, getting to his feet, "don't think for a moment that I am drunk: this is my ensign." He teeters toward Iago, who steadies his woozy lieutenant. "My right hand," he declares solemnly, putting his arm around Iago then puzzling over its reappearance on Iago's far shoulder. "And *this* is my left!" he laughs drunkenly and thrusts his far hand up in the air, Iago keeping him upright. "I am not drunk – I can stand well enough on my own, thank you," he says and pushes Iago away, "and I can speak well enough too…"

"Very well indeed!" one of the gentlemen from Cyprus teases as he uses a candle to light his pipe.

"All right then…" Cassio babbles, "you mustn't think I'm drunk, not drunk then, by a long…" His voice trailing off, he ambles aimlessly across the courtyard before heading inside, using the columns along the archway to hold himself up.

Back at the table, Montano downs the last of his wine and rises. "Duty calls, gentlemen. The first watch will be getting underway."

"You see this fellow who's just left us?" Iago asks as he pours more wine for the gentlemen from Cyprus. "He is a soldier fit to stand at Caesar's side and offer counsel. And yet…" Iago pauses long enough to catch Montano's undivided attention. "…he has a defect – nothing terrible, mind you, but a flaw that stands in contrast to all that is so admirable in him, as dark night stands out from bright day. 'Tis most unfortunate," he says gravely, "I worry that the trust Othello puts in him will, at a point when this infirmity's got the better of him, bring some catastrophe down upon the island."

"But is he often like this?" Montano asks.

Iago nods grimly. "Every night before he goes to bed: he'll stay awake around the clock if drink doesn't send him off to sleep."

"It might be a good idea to make the General aware of this. Perhaps he can't see it, or in his wisdom he values Cassio's abilities so highly, he overlooks his shortcomings. Is that not likely?"

But before Iago can respond, Roderigo charges into the courtyard.

"Roderigo – " Iago quickly excuses himself and rushes over. "He went in there!" Iago whispers sternly and points toward the archway. "Go after him!"

"In any case," Montano tells Iago when he returns, "it's a great pity the noble Moor would entrust the position of second-in-command to someone with what must be a deep-rooted problem. It would be wise for someone to raise the matter directly with the General."

"Well it won't be me," Iago replies hastily, "not for all the love on this fair island. I have a great deal of affection for Cassio – "

Cries of "Help! Help!" can be heard coming from within the archway corridor.

" – and would do anything to see him cured of his malady," Iago finishes. "But what in heaven's name is that noise?"

"God's blood, you wastrel! You weasel! You worm!" Cassio's violent insults get louder until he storms from the archway in pursuit of Roderigo, who streaks across the courtyard terrace and cowers behind Montano at first, but then ducks away to stand with Iago.

"What's this, lieutenant?" Montano demands of the sword-wielding Cassio.

"A worthless nobody tell me how to do my job? I'll carve him like a jack-o-lantern!"

"Carve me?" Roderigo squeals, terrified.

"Stop snivelling, you rat."

Montano corrals Cassio. "No, good lieutenant! I pray you, sir, put down your sword before someone is injured – "

"Let go of me, sir, or that will be you."

"Come, come," Montano responds patiently. "You're drunk."

"Drunk?" Cassio cries, offended, and lunges at Montano, who has no choice but to draw his sword and fight.

Iago shoos Roderigo away. "Get going – shout that a riot is breaking out!" He then turns back to Cassio and Montano, who are hard at it with clashing swords. "No, good lieutenant! For God's sake, gentlemen – Someone help! Lieutenant – Montano –Sirs – Help! Masters – this is a fine way to begin the nightly watch – "

The gong of a heavy bell being repeatedly struck fills the night air.

"Who's that ringing the bell?" Iago cries. "What the devil – the town will be up in arms! For God's sake, lieutenant, stop or you'll be completely disgraced!"

"What is the matter here?" Othello demands, striding into the courtyard flanked by a dozen soldiers and numerous attendants.

"God's death, I'm bleeding badly," Montano cries, clutching his side where Cassio has wounded him, "but I'll kill him before I die!" He musters his remaining strength and leaps at Cassio, who steps away from the jabbing sword but in the process smashes into a table so the candles and wine bottles go flying.

"Stop if you value your lives!" Othello commands as the bottles shatter on the courtyard clay tiles, red wine splashing on his soldiers' boots. He holds out an arm for them to stay put while he grapples with Montano himself and points for Iago to deal with Cassio.

"Restrain yourself, lieutenant!" Iago urges. "Sir – Montano – gentlemen – have you lost your senses? Stop, for heaven's sake, the General has ordered you both – "

"Hold on, hold on now," Othello says as he forces the fighters apart, Montano leaning on the General, Cassio pacing restlessly in front of Iago as if, oblivious to Othello's presence, he'll attack Montano again at the first opportunity. Othello glares sternly at both men in turn. "What's this all about? Have we decided to start slaughtering each other, which even the Turks are forbidden by their beliefs from doing? For goodness' sake cease this barbaric brawling or I warn him who makes the slightest move it will be his very last. And silence that dreadful bell!" he hollers, "the racket will send the island into a panic. Now, what is the problem, gentlemen?" Breathless and angry, neither

Montano nor Cassio will speak. "Honest Iago, your grief-stricken look says much. Tell me, as an honest friend, who started this row?"

Torn, Iago can only shake his head and offer a blank stare. "I don't know," he says in confusion, "it was all very friendly, but then…just now…we were talking quite cordially the way a bride and groom might when undressing for bed, but all of a sudden, as if something celestial had come down and taken over their bodies, these men had drawn their swords and begun going at one another in hot-blooded fury. I can't say how the senseless quarrel started—I only wish in some glorious battle I'd lost the legs that brought me here in the first place."

Othello studies his ensign with a dissatisfied frown before turning to the others.

"How did you come to forget yourself like this?" he asks Michael Cassio.

"Please believe me, General, when I tell you I have no idea." Still drunk, he straightens up and struggles to stand at attention, the growing magnitude of his misbehavior apparent in the increasingly somber look on his face.

"Worthy Montano," Othello says firmly, "you've always been known for your civility: ever since you were young, people have admired your even temper and your composure. You are highly spoken of by men of wise judgment. What can have happened that you would forsake your well deserved reputation and become involved in a vicious night brawl? Answer me." Clutching the bloody wound in his side, Montano makes his way over to a stool and sits down, slumping against the table.

"Worthy Othello, I am badly hurt," he says, wincing, " – your officer Iago can relate what happened – since my strength ebbs – it is painful now to speak of what I know, yet in truth I cannot grasp what I have said or done amiss tonight – unless to save myself was wrong – or fending off attack be now a sin – "

"Now by heaven!" Othello fumes in frustration, "bloody temper seeks to overrule most level-headed reason, and anger having clouded better judgment seeks to shake the truth from shadows where it hides – God's *blood*, if I so much as nod my head or raise this arm, even he of topmost rank will fall into obscurity. Let me know, right now, once and for all, how this disgraceful fight began, what prompted it, and though the guilty party had been born my very twin he shall be severed from me now. In this a strife-torn town, still reeling from the threat of all out war, what business did either of you have conducting here a private, personal broil? At night, within the courtyard, and while on duty looking out – as was to be – for public welfare? It's vile is what I say!" He wheels around and takes Iago by the jacket collar. "Who began this, ensign?"

Fading fast, Montano appeals to Iago. "If as a fellow army man you find yourself allied or bound to Cassio in telling more or less than what is true – then never can you call yourself a soldier."

"Don't talk of something that hits so close to home," Iago protests, " – I would rather have this tongue cut from my mouth than let it offend Michael Cassio and yet I know full well to speak the truth will do the man no harm. Thus, General, here is what transpired: Montano and I being in conversation, there came a fellow crying out for help because Lieutenant Cassio was chasing him with swinging sword and threatening what his blade would do. Sir, this gentleman," Iago says and motions toward Montano, "then steps in front of Cassio and entreats him not to strike, while I pursued the frightened, shrieking fellow in case his cries – as it so happened after all – might send the town's inhabitants into an outright panic. He, being more swift of foot, fled before I could stop him, and so I rushed back here for I made out the clang of clashing swords, as well as Cassio hurling bitter oaths, the likes of which until tonight I'd never heard before. Returning to the courtyard, for the interval was brief, I found them close together fiercely raining blows and thrusts on one another, just as when you parted them, sir. More than this I can't report. But men are men, the best sometimes forget; though Cassio did some slight wrong to him, as men in throes of anger sometimes strike at those that mean no harm, yet Cassio surely – and this I do believe – must have received from him who ran away some slurring insult which his dignity could simply not abide."

"I know, Iago, your loyalty and friendship make light of things for Cassio's sake," Othello says, and turns to face his lieutenant. "I hold you close to my heart, Michael Cassio, but no longer can you serve as second officer – Look," he interrupts himself, gazing over Cassio's shoulder, "if my gentle love has not been awakened!" Iago is the only one besides Othello who glances at Desdemona moving through the courtyard toward them. Lowering his eyes, Othello gives Cassio a curt frown. "I'll have to make an example of you before the men – "

"What is the matter, dear?" Desdemona asks as she arrives and stands beside her husband.

"All is well, sweetheart," Othello assures her, "come back to bed. – Sir," he addresses Montano, "I will personally see to your wounds." He motions some of his soldiers to assist Montano. "In the meantime, I need you to keep a careful eye on the situation, Iago, and calm any who might have been frightened by this inexcusable episode." Iago inclines his head, accepting the General's order. "Come Desdemona," Othello says tenderly and steers his wife toward the covered archway, "this is what comes with being a soldier – having one's nightly slumber disturbed when duty calls…"

When the others have gone, a glum-looking Cassio throws himself down on the stool where, by coincidence, he recently sat drinking. He stares intently at the still burning candles, two wine bottles and several drinking cups…until in a sudden violent motion he clears the table top with a swipe of his arm.

Iago peers down at the mess of pewter, broken glass and a pool of red wine not far from his feet. He crouches down and picks up the single candle that has continued to burn.

"You're hurt lieutenant…"

"Yes," Cassio snaps, "more than I can bear."

"Surely there's something – "

"Reputation, reputation, reputation!" Cassio wails despondently. "I have lost my reputation, lost the very soul of my being – and what remains isn't worth salvaging. My reputation, Iago, my reputation!"

Iago pulls up a stool and takes a seat, staring at the candle flame. "In all honesty I thought you had received a bodily wound," he says matter-of-factly. "There's more to worry about with that, than with reputation. Reputation is a useless and contrived thing, usually acquired without merit and lost without deserving. You haven't lost a reputation at all, unless you consider yourself its loser. Why, man, there are ways to win back the General. At the moment he has cast you aside in anger, a punishment more about policy than personal feeling – he needs to show authority over the men in his command. Beg him to grant you a pardon and he'll relent."

"I would rather beg to be despised than to have let down so good a commander through such reckless and contemptible behavior – conduct completely unbecoming an officer. Drunken babbling? squabbling? Quarreling, swearing, and ranting senselessly against my own shadow? If the invisible power of wine had a name I would say it must be Satan!"

"Who was it you chased with your sword?" Iago asks and gets to his feet. "What had he done to you?"

Cassio shakes his head. "I have no idea."

"None whatsoever?"

"I remember a number of things, but nothing very clearly. I quarreled, but I can't say why. O God, that men so blithely put what's bad for them in their mouths and let it steal away their brains! – That with joy, pleasure, revelry and celebration we turn ourselves into wild animals!"

"But wait lieutenant, you are sober enough now: how have you been able to recover so fast?"

Cassio heaves a remorseful sigh. "The devil Drunkenness yields to the devil Anger. One imperfection clears the way for the other and I'm left despising myself in both respects."

"Come now, you're too severe a judge of your own behavior. As far as things stand at this time, and in circumstances like this, we could all wish none of this had happened. But it has, so for your own good you must try to mend things."

In spite of Iago's efforts at encouragement, Cassio continues to wear an expression of somber dismay. "If I ask him for my position back he will tell me I'm a drunkard: even if I had all the mouths of many-headed Hydra pleading on my behalf, such an answer would silence them all. To be considered a sensible man one moment, then nothing but a drunken lout the next! How strange…a few drinks too many and before you know it the devil is going down the hatch with each cup consumed."

"Now, now. Wine can be a good friend if it's used properly: stop railing against it. And, good lieutenant, bear in mind that I too am your friend."

"Truly, you have been until now. But my being drunk…?"

Iago dismisses Cassio's concern with a wave of his hand. "You or any man alive may get drunk from time to time." He returns to his stool and sits down again, leaning in toward Cassio as though prepared to have a heart-to-heart talk. "I'll tell you what you need to do," he says decisively, then glances around the courtyard to make sure they're alone. "The General's wife is now the General, if you see what I'm saying…"

Cassio doesn't and shakes his head.

"Well, what I mean is this: the General is now so smitten with and absorbed in the contemplation, observation and appreciation of his lovely wife's charms and remarkable physical favors, that if you give her an honest explanation of the situation you find yourself in and solicit her help in regaining your position…" Iago snaps his fingers. "You see? Besides, hers is such a generous, willing and I might even say – " Searching for the right word, he remembers an earlier conversation with Roderigo: " – such a *blessedly good* disposition, that she calls into question her own goodness if she can't give people more help than they ask for. This break between you and her husband, ask her to splint the two of you back together, so to speak – and I'll lay my fortune against any bet you could venture to make that this fracture in your friendship will not only be healed, but end up making the two of you closer than you were before."

"That sounds like very good advice," Cassio nods, his face brightening.

"I offer it in a spirit of true friendship and genuine affection," Iago says warmly and extends his hand to Cassio.

"And I accept it without reservation," Cassio responds respectfully, giving Iago's hand a hearty shake. "Early tomorrow morning," he says with eager enthusiasm, "I will approach the virtuous Desdemona about taking up my case with the General. After all, my career is doomed if tonight's decision stands."

"You're doing the right thing without question," Iago says. "Goodnight now, lieutenant. I must go on watch as the General instructed."

"Of course. Good night, honest Iago." He insists on shaking Iago's hand once more and then departs, leaving Iago at the table by himself with the flickering candle. He holds it sideways. Spreading the fingers of his free hand on the table, he lets melting wax drip carefully onto his fingernails, one at a time...

"Who dares accuse me of being a villain when I merely dispense good, honest advice – offering a splendid course of action for winning over the Moor, and one which couldn't be more in accord with how the General thinks. It's nothing at all to persuade the sympathetic Desdemona to go along with any slightly reasonable request – that's the way she *is*: born without an ungenerous bone in that body of hers, which can win over the Moor in the blink of an eye, unlike anything I could do or say – why, he's so enthralled with this wife of his he'd renounce his own holy baptism, even the prospect of heavenly redemption, if it meant pleasing her."

Iago takes a moment to admire the work he's done on one set of fingernails before switching the candle to his other hand so he can wax the remaining five.

"She can do *this*, do *that*, do *anything* she likes, and her most fanciful wish is his absolute command. How am I a villain," he demands, "when I'm advising Cassio to do no more than take advantage of a similar helplessness on her part about doing good, which in turn brings the desired benefit to him. Great God in hell," he reasons, "when evildoers commit their blackest sins they do so under the pretext of having the best intentions, as I do now." He sits up, a self-satisfied grin spreading over his lips. "While this gullible fool presses Desdemona to revive his fortunes, and she in turn implores the Moor to change his mind about reducing Cassio to the ranks, I'll bend his ear with a scathing lie: that she's only trying to have Cassio reinstated because she lusts after him. And the more she continues to plead the disgraced man's case, the more she makes the Moor distrust her motives – why," he smirks bitterly, "I will turn that lily-white virtue of hers to blackest tar and let her own goodness be the net that entangles them all."

Blowing out the candle, he is busy watching the thin column of smoke as it rises from the wick, when Roderigo reappears. "How now, Roderigo?"

He heaves a weary sigh. "I'm following along in the chase," he says morosely, "but I'm far from the lead hounds – merely one in the rear barking up the wrong tree it always seems. My money is almost gone. I have been badly roughed up." He indicates his torn clothes, a bleeding cut on his arm and bruising under both his eyes. "The upshot is that I have some hard-earned experience to show for my ordeal, but not much else. I'm nearly broke, Iago, so I'm listening to the last of my common sense and heading back to Venice."

"How unfortunate are those who have no patience," Iago laments cooly. "What wound ever healed other than with time? You get what you want in life through wisdom, not witchcraft, my friend, and wisdom only comes with the passing of time. Don't you see? Cassio beat you, but through that small hurt you have beaten Cassio. He's been dismissed, has he not? Though other things might seem to be growing best in the bright sunlight, remember it's those which blossom first that ripen before the rest. That is to say: others may be growing in Desdemona's eyes at the moment, but your efforts are blossoming nicely and will bear fruit when the time is ripe. Hold your horses, wait just a bit longer." Iago notices that dawn is breaking, orange light spreading in the eastern sky. "Good lord, it's almost morning. This revelry and excitement has made the hours pass quickly. Retire for now. Go back to your room. Run along, Roderigo. We'll know more later on."

Dead tired, dispirited and sore, Roderigo eyes one of the stools and moves to sit down but Iago shoots to his feet and stands him up. "No more of this – get on your way, man!" He walks Roderigo part way across the courtyard and points to the covered archway.

Alone, Iago surveys the mess that has been made in the courtyard. He walks over to the fountain, cups his hands under the jet of water streaming from the stone Neptune, and drinks.

"Two things now remain," he says, wiping his mouth. "My wife must appeal to her mistress on behalf of Cassio, I'll arrange for that. Meanwhile I'll take the Moor aside and have him discover Cassio as he pleads desperately for Desdemona's help. Yes!" he exclaims, "that's just the way: dull not the plot with lackluster delay!"

3.1

Early the next morning, Cassio moves hastily through the castle's main hall with a group of musicians. Pale and disheveled, he still wears the soiled and wine-stained clothes he had on the night before. Muttering to himself, he glances around the area at the foot of the grand staircase, looking for the ideal place to station the musicians.

"Masters, play here," he says when he finally decides on a location. "I will reward you for your trouble. Now, give me something short, but which bids the General a most pleasant 'good morning'…"

The musicians arrange themselves as instructed, tuning the strings of their lutes and viols to a note played by a man on the recorder. The fellow with the tabor tamps idly on his drum until the rest are ready. The ensemble then begins to play, however the sound carries over to a window alcove where a jester is sleeping, his red, blue and green fool's cap pulled low over his eyes. He is awakened by the music in no time and gets up, the bells on the points of his cap jingling as he marches over to the musicians.

Annoyed, he pinches his nostrils so that his voice has an irritating nasal tone. "Why, masters," he complains over the music, "your instruments sound like they've got bad colds, do your hear me? Bad colds!"

"What's that?" the man playing the lute demands, offended. "What are you talking about?"

The music comes to a stop while the jester, his voice normal, addresses the man with the recorder.

"This is a wind instrument you're playing, is it not?"

"Indeed, sir, it is."

"Well then, thereby hangs the tail."

"Whereby hangs the tail, sir?" the man asks, puzzled.

"The tail," says the jester, pointing to his behind. "Where the best wind music is made, sir." He promptly turns his back on the musicians and farts mischievously. The musicians groan, make faces and step back in disgust.

"But really, masters, here's some money for you," the jester explains and takes a handful of pennies from a little pouch he has with him. "Because the General so admires your music that he requests you, for love of a good tune, accept a small token of his appreciation and go elsewhere to share it with others."

"Well, sir, we will not," the recorder player says defiantly.

Cassio, who has gone part way up the stairs to hear how the music sounds, comes back down to see why it has stopped.

Shaking his head at the musicians, the jester folds his arms and sighs. "All right, if you have some music that *can't* be heard," he says patiently, "he might be agreeable if you gave that a try. Because in truth, music and the General don't mix, as they say."

While the musicians frown, scratch their heads and question each other, Cassio throws the jester a worried look.

"You mean – " he starts to say.

"We don't have any music like that," the recorder player tells the jester.

"Like what?" the jester asks.

"That can't be heard."

"Oh. Then if I were you I'd pack up your pluckers, your blowers and your beaters, and begone. Go. Vanish. Into thin air. Foof!" the jester says, gesturing with his hand like it's a wizard's wand. He tosses his money pouch at the recorder player, who checks that there's money inside and then gives the signal for his fellow musicians to disperse.

"Would my honest friend let me have a word?" Cassio asks.

"I don't know," the jester jokes, "you'd best ask your honest friend."

"Now, sir, please let's not quibble," Cassio says anxiously and takes out a coin. "There's a good piece of gold in return for a favor – if the woman attending to the General's wife seems to have roused herself, would you be good enough to tell her there's someone by the name of Cassio who begs a word with her. Would you do this for me?"

The jester looks Cassio over, a mocking smile playing on his lips.

"She is a-roused, sir," the jester winks rudely. "If she seems a-roused enough to come down here, I will let her know someone who is a-roused himself, wishes to talk with her."

"Please do so, my good friend." Cassio hands over the gold coin. Accepting it, the jester puts it between his teeth and bites down to make sure it's the genuine article. Satisfied, he turns and makes his way out of the hall, passing Iago, who's on his way in.

"Ensign!" Cassio calls, "what good timing."

His face showing no expression, Iago looks Cassio up and down.

"I take it you haven't been to bed."

"As a matter of fact, no," Cassio admits self-consciously. "When we parted it was almost daybreak – but listen, Iago," he says excitedly. "I've been bold and sent for your wife, to see if she will arrange for me to meet with Desdemona – "

"I'll send the worthy lady to you presently. And devise a way of keeping the Moor occupied so the two of you can talk about matters more freely."

"Many thanks," Cassio says, flashing a grateful smile. Iago gives him a quick pat on the back and goes toward the stairs. "I've never known a man more kind and thoughtful," Cassio remarks to himself as he watches Iago ascend to the second floor and disappear through a large set of doors.

"Good morning, lieutenant," Emilia says, coming up behind Cassio. "I'm very sorry to hear of your trouble, but all will be well I'm sure. The General and his wife have been discussing matters and I know she speaks vigorously for you. The Moor feels that because this Montano you wounded is so revered in Cyprus and has such strong affiliations here, it would be wise for him to refuse your request for reinstatement right now. He insists that he is very fond of you and says it is this high personal regard which will allow him to bring you in again when the first suitable opportunity presents itself."

"Even so, could I possibly – if it's not asking too much – have a few moments alone with Desdemona?"

Emilia considers for a moment: sees the state of his clothes, the distress in his handsome but haggard face…

Her mind made up, she gives him a sympathetic nod. "Come along then. I will take you to a place where you will be able to speak privately with her."

"Thank you," Cassio says…

Officers, aides and attendants follow Othello along a corridor that opens onto the castle rotunda. The General is all business as he accepts some sealed documents from his scribe and passes them to Iago.

"Give these letters to the captain of my ship and have him convey them to the Senate, along with my personal respects, once he arrives in Venice. After that, come back and meet me up top. We'll be walking on the ramparts."

"Very well, my lord. I shall take care of it."

"Gentlemen, the ramparts…"

"Whenever you're ready, your lordship," the officer who has taken Cassio's place replies and signals his men to move out.…

For a few moments the only sound in the courtyard comes from the stream of water the trident-bearing statue of Neptune pours into the fountain pool. But with the arrival of Emilia and Desdemona, birds frisking on the statue's head suddenly scatter and fly off. The two women walk briskly toward a garden beyond the courtyard: tall cypress and pine trees, quartz paths, vivid yellow, blue and red flowers, where Cassio is waiting.

Desdemona has Emilia stay with her as she approaches and greets the disgraced lieutenant. "Rest assured, good Cassio, that I am doing everything I can to help you."

"And a good thing, madam," Emilia chimes in. "I swear the matter has my husband upset as if it had happened to him."

"Your husband is a true friend, Emilia," Desdemona acknowledges, then turns toward Cassio. "You mustn't doubt for a minute that I will have my husband and you back to being friends again, as you were before now."

"Gracious madam, despite what happens to Michael Cassio, he will be forever grateful to you."

"I know, and I thank you. There is a long standing kinship between my husband and you – you have been the best of companions. Therefore be confident, Cassio, that the current estrangement is no more than a wise political move your General has little choice in making."

"Perhaps that is so, but good lady such a move could stand for a long while, or gradually fade away unnoticed, or be subject to the whims of changing circumstance, so that by being absent and my place occupied by someone else, my General would forget my unbounded devotion and loyalty to him."

Touched by Cassio's words, Desdemona shakes her head in protest.

"Don't let yourself think that: here, in Emilia's presence, I promise with all my heart you will have your place again." She reaches out and takes his hands in hers. "Know, too, that when I make a vow for a friend I never go back on my word. My lord Othello shall never rest but I'll keep him awake nights till he's out of sorts, I'll busy him with talking about this in bed and at mealtimes – during everything he does – constantly reminding him of your desire to be restored as his officer again: therefore be content, Cassio, for your solicitor would rather die than abandon your case."

Cassio brings Desdemona's right hand up to his lips and kisses it, unaware that Iago and Othello are crossing the courtyard in full view of the garden.

"Madam," Emilia says, "here comes my lord."

Suddenly uncomfortable, Cassio tries removing his hands from Desdemona's.

"Madam, I'll be on my way…"

"Why no, stay and talk to me a while longer," she tells him tenderly and keeps hold of his hands.

"Madam, not now," Cassio says nervously and pulls his hands free. "I'm most ill at ease – it's not right for one in my position – "

"Do as you see fit, then," she says and watches him leave through a different part of the garden.

"I don't like the look of that," Iago mutters to himself but loud enough for Othello to hear as they walk through the courtyard that gives onto the garden.

"Don't like the look of what?"

Iago shrugs evasively. "Nothing my lord, or if – I don't really know," he says and abruptly stops talking.

Othello stops walking and gazes toward the garden.

"Wasn't that Cassio who just parted from my wife?"

"Cassio, my lord? No, surely not. I can't imagine him making away so guilty-like upon seeing you."

"I do believe it was he," Othello maintains and heads into the garden.

Iago nods to his wife Emilia as he passes, but carries on behind Othello and takes up a position close by. He makes a show of glancing to the other end of the garden, and, satisfied that Cassio has left, turns to admiring the beauty of the flowers.

"Hello, my lord," Desdemona says, greeting her husband with an affectionate kiss on the cheek. "I have been talking with a suitor here," she teases, "a man who languishes in your disfavor."

"And who would that be?"

"Why, your lieutenant, Cassio."

Othello exchanges a knowing look with Iago.

"Indeed, my lord," Desdemona continues in earnest, "were I in possession of the power to charm and convince you, I would push for his immediate reinstatement: because if he isn't someone truly devoted to you – whose mistake was a mere matter of bad judgment and in no way deliberate – then I am no judge of character. Please, could you have him recalled?"

"This *suitor*, as you put it, who departed just now?" Othello says lightly.

"Yes, but believe me he is so distraught over this business that he has left part of his sorrow with me so I can bear a little of his burden of grief. Dear love, could you see that he is restored to office?"

"Not now, sweet Desdemona, perhaps some other time."

"But soon?"

"Sooner, my sweet, for you…"

"Will it be by supper tonight?"

"No, not tonight."

"Tomorrow dinner, then?"

"I won't be dining at home tomorrow. I meet my captains at a gathering here at the castle."

Bothered by her persistence, Othello avoids looking at her directly.

"What about tomorrow night then?" she asks, coming around so she's facing him. Othello shakes his head. "Or Tuesday morning?" He shakes his head. "Or Tuesday noon or night?" He backs away, shaking his head. Desdemona pursues him. "Wednesday? Perhaps Wednesday?" This time Othello shrugs. "Just name a time," she pesters, "but please don't let it be more than three days. You know he's guilt-ridden and growing despondent over an offence that people with common sense – except those, of course, who claim the military *must make examples of their best for the discipline of the rest* – hold as an unfortunate mistake, for which a private reprimand would more than suffice. When will he be able to come to you and discuss this? Tell me, Othello." The General gazes in the direction Cassio went upon leaving the garden…

"I wonder in my heart," Desdemona says disappointedly, "what you could ever ask of me that I would deny, or keep you harping on about, as I am now? This is Michael Cassio, my lord: he who convinced you to woo me when so many others had tried to win my heart but failed – who, whenever I spoke in the least critical way about you, came immediately to your defense. Is it so hard to bring him back into favor?" she demands. "Especially when he is owed so much – "

"Please, no more," Othello protests. "Let him come to me whenever he wishes. I cannot deny you a favor."

"Very well," Desdemona says, surprised but happy with his sudden acquiescence. "Although," she clarifies, "this is not a favor, strictly speaking. It's more as if I've pointed out the benefit of something to you – having you appreciate something that will be good for you."

His back to her, Othello listens as Desdemona continues to press her point.

"No, when I have a suit whereby I mean to test your love, it shall require deep and careful thought, and be suitably daunting for you to grant, not a matter like this – "

"I will deny you nothing," Othello repeats, "for which reason I ask in return that you give me a moment to myself."

This unexpected request causes her to hesitate a moment. "Shall I deny you?" she then resumes, with a bright and amused smile. "Of course not! Farewell, my love."

"Farewell, Desdemona," he says, accepting her kiss on the cheek. "I'll be with you straight away…"

When Desdemona has left the garden, Emilia, on the verge of going, glares at Iago since he has made no move to depart. He puts a finger quickly to his lips then indicates Othello, deliberating in silence a short distance off.

"Emilia, come," Desdemona calls and waits for her to go on ahead into the courtyard before she turns back to Othello.

"Whatever thoughts your imagination has you believing," she states plainly, "for better or for worse, I am a faithful wife…"

With that she is gone, Othello, still with his back to Iago, brooding quietly.

"Astounding!" he exclaims, a beaming smile on his face as he turns toward Iago. "Altogether astounding – damnation take my soul if I don't love this woman to the depths, and if ever I were to stop, my world would be left full shattered."

"My noble lord – " Iago says, speaking up.

"What's that Iago?" the General inquires, distracted by his private musings.

"Did Michael Cassio, when you were wooing my lady that is, did he know of the love you felt?"

"Of course he did, from the very outset. Why do you ask?"

"No reason. Just satisfying my curiosity."

"About what?"

"I didn't think he and your wife were acquainted with one another…"

"Oh yes, the three of us were often together."

"Indeed?"

Othello frowns and makes a face. "'Indeed'? You make it sound as though there's something strange – why, Cassio's one of the most trustworthy people I know."

"Trustworthy, my lord?"

"'Trustworthy'? Yes, he's trustworthy."

"As far as anyone is…" Iago says evenly, though it's clear he has his doubts.

"Well, what do you think?"

"Think, my lord?"

"'Think, my lord?'" Othello asks in exasperation. "For heaven's sake, you're parroting everything I say like there's something on your mind you'd rather not talk about. You must mean something or else you wouldn't have said you didn't like it that Cassio walked away from my wife when he saw us coming – what didn't you like? And when I told you he advised me and stood by me when I was wooing Desdemona, you put on a perturbed frown as if there was something weighing upon your conscience when you blurted out 'Indeed?' Tell me, if you're a good friend, what's on your mind."

"My lord, you know I'm a good friend."

"I consider you so. And it's because I respect you as a man of integrity and trust, who chooses his words carefully before speaking, that I find these hesitations of yours disconcerting. They're a common trick among those who practice treachery, whereas for the righteous man they are astute, cautious considerations in which reason rather than emotion prevails."

Iago shrugs. "As for Michael Cassio then, I could swear to his honesty, I think."

"I think so too."

"Men should be what they seem, or be nothing at all."

"Rightly said, men should be what they seem."

"So I'm inclined to say Cassio's an honest man."

"No – I can tell there's more to this: let me hear what you have to say, Iago, what's really going through your mind – and put blunt thoughts into blunt words if you must."

"Begging your pardon, my lord. Though I am bound to you in all my duties, I am not bound to do that which even slaves are free from doing – expressing their innermost private thoughts. Why, what if they were downright malicious and untrue? We all know there isn't a good person alive into whose mind a little bad doesn't sometimes intrude. And who has a heart so pure that some evil notion doesn't at one time or another sit together with lawful thoughts in the court of conscience?"

"You undermine our friendship if you think something is wrong yet you refuse to talk to me about it," Othello says, growing annoyed.

Iago thinks about what he should do.

"I have to ask though, sir," he relents cautiously, "that since I can occasionally be mistaken in my assumptions – my penchant for snooping sometimes goes too far – your good judgment shouldn't rely overly much on what it hears from one who has such a vivid imagination as I. What *would* be wrong, is if you worked yourself into a temper based on a few scattered and uncertain observations I made. Besides the fact they could be dangerous to your peace of mind, they could disastrously effect my reputation as a man of honesty and good sense, if I simply came out and let you know whatever I was thinking."

"Bloody hell, what does that mean?" Othello demands.

"Only that whether in man or woman, reputation is the most precious thing a person possesses. Someone who steals my money steals very little – it's something..." he throws a look at one flower, "but it's nothing," he says, looking at another. He slips out his money pouch and stares at Othello. "It was mine," he tosses the pouch, "now it's his."

Catching the pouch, Othello realizes it's empty. Iago takes it back.

"Who will be enslaved by it, along with the wide world? – But someone who robs me of my good name robs me of something that can't make him a penny richer but makes me poor as can be."

Othello seizes him by the front of his jacket. "I swear I will find out what you're thinking – "

" – Even if you held my heart in your hand?" Iago smiles, "which you won't as long as it's in my keeping – "

"Ha!" cries Othello and throws him to the ground.

Iago scrambles to get back on his feet. "Beware of jealousy, my lord," he taunts as he straightens his jacket. "… The green-eyed monster that toys with the heart it feeds on. The cheated husband lives in bliss who knows his wife has been unfaithful but loves her no more, yet how damnably slow the minutes seem to pass for him who dotes though he doubts, suspects though he still strongly loves!"

"Misery…" Othello murmurs.

"A poor man is rich if he has peace of mind, as rich as he could ever want to be, but boundless riches leave a man cold if he constantly fears becoming poor. Dear Lord," Iago says, crossing himself reverently, "protect the hearts of men everywhere from jealousy."

"Why – why are you saying this? You think I would let jealousy become my life, each week bringing with it fresh new suspicions? No: if I ever have doubts I will face them directly. I'll not have my days and nights destroyed by mischievous rumors and wild speculations which, according to you, dog the jealous man. Indeed, it doesn't make me jealous in the least to hear people say my wife is beautiful, charming and sociable, and that she sings, plays and dances superbly. These virtues only enrich her other gifts. Nor, in respect of my own deficiencies within society, will I feel threatened enough to question her fidelity – she had eyes to see and chose me. No, Iago, I am someone who must see with his own eyes before he can believe. If I have no doubt, what is there that can be proved? And in the absence of something to be proved, how can there be guilt? I say this is all pointless: proof for jealousy or for love is always in the putting."

Believing the conversation over, Othello begins moving back through the garden. Iago wastes no time catching up but stays a step behind the General.

"I am happy to hear this, my lord!" he explains, "for now I can be a true friend and dutiful servant in frank and honest fashion…"

Othello slows down but keeps walking.

"Though I speak without proof," Iago says in a confidential tone, "yet I'm duty-bound to tell you this."

Othello halts and turns.

"Watch your wife closely, especially when she's with Cassio. But observe her in such a way that you don't appear too suspicious on the one hand or too trusting on the other. I could not stand to see your valiant and kind-hearted goodness abused: keep your eye on her is what I recommend. I'm very familiar with the games these Venetians play – they let God see pranks and mischief they hide from their husbands at all costs, for in their minds what matters most is not whether what they're doing is right or wrong, but whether they get caught doing it."

"And you believe this about Desdemona?"

"She deceived her father in order to marry you, did she not? And those times she trembled in fear and shivered in awe of your appearance, was she not at the same moment most passionately enthralled?"

"So she was."

"There you are, then: one who so young could be so good at keeping up appearances that even her own father was left in the dark to her purposes – little wonder the poor man thought he'd lost his daughter to sorcery and witchcraft. But I am largely at fault here, I humbly beg your pardon for being so devoted in conversation about this..." He turns away and hangs his head as if ashamed.

Othello puts a hand on Iago's shoulder. "Nonsense, I am forever in your debt."

"I see this is troubling for you," Iago says, looking up.

"Not a bit, no..."

"I hope it isn't... I hope too you know that every word I've said comes from my heart. But, I can see you *are* troubled – I can't have you put what I've said down to anything greater than what is, for now, mere suspicion."

"I would not do that."

"Good, but if somehow you *were* to, my lord, what I've said would have brought about a terrible misunderstanding: Cassio's a most trusted friend."

Othello gazes off.

"My lord," Iago says, concerned, "again I see you're troubled."

"No, not at all. I don't believe Desdemona is anything less than a good and faithful wife."

"May she always continue to be – and may you always continue believing she is."

Iago keeps his eyes trained warily on the General, who ponders this last remark intently...

"And yet," Othello says, "human nature does have its stray moments of weakness."

"Indeed it does, sir, and if I may be so bold as to say, rejecting the many marriage proposals she received from gentlemen of her own social rank and standing – which is the natural and preferred course in matters of this…complexion – bah! It reeks of uncontrollable whim, unnatural and, some might say, abnormal craving…"

Again, Othello looks away. "But forgive me, sir," Iago insists, "I'm not for a moment putting forward these thoughts about your wife herself, though I have to wonder if, steeped in desire as she is, she could awake one day and begin comparing you with the men she turned down, and regret what she'd done."

"Farewell for now," Othello says, ignoring Iago's comment. "If you come across something more, let me know: it would not go amiss to have your wife keep an eye on her as well. Leave me…"

"My lord," Iago says formally and backs away from Othello, "I do take my leave." He moves off slowly along the same path Cassio took.

Closing his eyes, Othello heaves a weary sigh. He rubs his eyes and, on opening them again to take in the balmy garden breeze, glances at two red-winged black birds chasing each other in and among the flowers.

"Why did I marry?" he wonders quietly as he paces slowly about. "This vigilant fellow both sees and knows more – much more – than he lets on – "

"My lord," Iago interrupts, having lingered nearby. He hastens back to Othello with a look of serious worry on his face. "If I might, I would urge you to look into this business *no* further. Let time do its work. Although it's only proper that Cassio have his position back – since he brings to it unquestionable abilities – at the same time if it were possible to hold off a little while on your decision, you would be able to study his behavior: noticing whether or not your lady often insists upon seeing him. Much can be discerned from that. In the meantime, just think of me as putting my nose in where it doesn't belong – which, goodness knows, I have a tendency to do – and let her innocence stand, I beseech you, my lord."

"Fear not my handling of it," Othello says.

"I once more take my leave then," Iago replies, noticing as he goes that Desdemona and Emilia have returned to the courtyard and are making their way toward the garden once more.

His brows narrowed in pensive thought, Othello resumes pacing and then abruptly stops. "This fellow's wisely perceptive and knows much, his mind attuned to the ways of human behavior. If I were to discover my wife has thrown off the ties by which we have been bound, though it breaks my very heart, I would have to cast her aside and leave her to fend for herself, to roam where fortune wills. Perhaps because I am black and have not the genteel discourse that her gallant crowd employs, or that I'm further along in years – though not by much – I am cheated upon…my only relief to be the loathing of her. So much for this curse of marriage…that we can call these fair creatures ours but not their desires! I would rather be a toad living on dungeon vapors than let a corner of the one I love be used by others. Yet it is the bane of those in high position, I suppose, not to be spared having adulterous wives, as poorer men are. It must be destined, even as our growing old, that we are to know at some point along our way the piercing horns of their infidelity."

At the sound of women's laughter, Othello turns his eyes toward the courtyard: Desdemona and Emilia are entering the garden.

"Here she is," he mutters as the women advance. "If she has been unfaithful, then heaven mocks itself – I cannot believe it…"

Desdemona darts inquisitive glances around the garden, thinking her husband was talking to someone. Satisfied he is alone, she kisses him affectionately on the cheek.

"Are you ready, my dear Othello? Lunch, and the island dignitaries you invited to join you, are waiting."

"Of course," he murmurs softly.

"Why is your voice so quiet and subdued? Are you not well?"

"I have a headache coming on," he says, rubbing his brow.

"No doubt because you haven't been sleeping well. It will pass soon enough." She plucks a handkerchief from her sleeve, white with small strawberry clusters embroidered on it, and starts to dab his perspiring black forehead. "Let me see if I can ease the pain – "

He seizes her by the wrist and throws off her hand. "Never mind. Come, we'll go inside to the guests."

"I am terribly sorry you're not feeling well," Desdemona says, confused, as they walk off arm in arm, Emilia hurrying over to retrieve the white handkerchief lying in among the flowers where it fell. She puts it up to her cheek and luxuriates in its exquisite softness.

"I am glad to have found you," she says, talking to herself, "for you were her first keepsake from the Moor. My stubborn husband has been pestering me for ages to lay my hands on you, but I know my lady treasures you so – the Moor entreated her to keep you as proof of his abiding love – she makes sure you are never out of her possession so she can kiss you and talk to you when she and the Moor are apart." She admires the stitched strawberry clusters. "I'll have this needlework removed and give you to Iago: heaven only knows what he'll do with you, certainly I don't, but having you will do something to satisfy this latest whim – "

"How now!" Iago calls and slips out from behind a nearby bank of flowers, startling Emilia so she lets out a frightened whimper.

"What are you doing here by yourself?" he asks, walking forward.

"You're one to talk. Besides, I have something for you – " she says and whisks the white handkerchief behind her back.

"Something for me…" Iago murmurs, apparently indifferent, but thrusts out his hand and lunges behind her just the same. Too quick for him, his wife blocks the attempt. Iago's hand ends up buried in the folds of dress between her legs. "It's the most common thing in the world," he says when she bats his hand away.

"What is?"

"To have a foolish wife."

"Is that so? Well, what will you give your foolish wife for a particular handkerchief?"

"What handkerchief?"

"'What handkerchief?'" she teases and steps back when he tries once more to reach behind her back. "Why, the one the Moor gave Desdemona as a gift – which you were always after me to steal."

"You've stolen it from her?" he asks, his face brightening with excitement.

"No, as a matter of fact she let it drop by mistake and being right there, I took advantage of the situation and picked it up. See?" she says, holding up the white handkerchief and waving it proudly in his face.

"Good girl, let's have it," he says and tries snatching it but she puts it behind her back again.

"What will you do with it, having been so insistent that I pilfer it for you?"

Iago looks away. "What difference does it make?" he says callously, then moves fast and grabs her free arm, wrenching it fiercely until with a pained "Ow!" she brings the other hand forward and offers up the handkerchief.

"If it's not for some good cause then give it back," Emilia protests. "The poor woman – she'll be frantic when she realizes it's gone."

"Play dumb in front of her – I need it. Now go, leave me be."

Rubbing her arm, which is red and sore where her husband twisted it, Emilia reluctantly obeys and leaves the garden.

"I'll plant it in Cassio's quarters so that he discovers it," Iago says with a menacing smile. He appraises the handkerchief and tosses it gleefully in the air, grinning as he watches it float lightly down into his outstretched hand. "To the jealous mind the smallest trifles can be as convincing as hard evidence. This could prove most helpful. The Moor has already grown uneasy with the hints I've let drop: most lethal to the active imagination are thoughts which at first burn harmlessly enough but with some careful fanning can be set blazing, the flames impossible to douse. " – Speak of the devil, and here he comes. " He spots Othello striding toward the garden, looking irate. "Neither opium nor other drugs narcotic," he gloats, his lips curling in a snide grin, " – nor all the sleeping potions in the world will ever treat you to the sweet sleep you enjoyed but yesterday…"

A livid Othello comes storming into the garden and confronts Iago.

"You! Why did you get me thinking so?"

He takes Iago in his clutches and yanks him close with such force the ensign is standing on his tiptoes.

"Now, now, General, what's this?" he asks in a light, bemused voice, his shoulders hunched in Othello's rough grip.

"You know well what I say."

"I do not, General," he pleads.

Othello glares straight into Iago's eyes as if he's ready to break his neck. "Begone," he snarls a tense moment later and flings Iago aside. "Out of my sight – you've set me on the torturing rack. I swear it would be better knowing how badly I've been deceived than merely imagining I have been."

Picking himself up and brushing off his clothes, Iago inquires: "How is that, my lord?"

"What went on in my mind about her stolen hours of lust before now?" Othello demands. "I saw it not, thought it not, it harmed me not, I slept the night well, ate well, was happy and content as a man could be." He moves away from Iago and along the garden path as he talks. "I found no kisses from Cassio lingering on her lips. At least the man who's robbed, if he doesn't care about what's stolen and moreover if he's never told about it – he hasn't been robbed at all."

"I'm sorry to hear you talk this way," Iago tells him.

Othello takes a deep breath, regards a bevy of white orchids growing beside him with a concentrated stare.

"I would have been better off knowing that my whole army had been with her than not knowing whether any one of them had been. From now on I must say farewell to peace of mind, farewell contentment, farewell the troops in battle colors arrayed upon the field, marching with their dreams of victory. Farewell – farewell the charging steed and the bugle's shrill blast signaling triumph, the brave beat of advancing drums, the high, piercing whistle of the fife, the crested flags and color-resplendent banners, the pride, pomp and pageantry of glorious war! And, too, the deadly cannon, whose flaming mouths clamor and thunder loud as angry Jove himself. Farewell: Othello's life is over…"

"But can you be sure of this, my lord?" Iago asks innocently.

His turmoil all Iago's doing, Othello catches him by the throat and begins to squeeze.

"You will *make* me sure, villain. Prove my wife a whore, make me certain of it, give me visible proof," he warns, squeezing Iago's neck harder so that the ensign begins choking. "Or damn your eternal soul, it would be better for you to have been born a dog than defend yourself against my awakened wrath!"

"Has it come to this?" Iago croaks, his face growing pale for lack of air.

"Let me see it with my own eyes, or at least give me that proof on which no shred of smallest doubt could hang – or I will have your life!"

"My honored lord – " Iago's voice is no more than a rasping whisper.

Othello tightens his grip. "If you are doing this to slander her and torture me, don't even think to pray, abandon any thought of forgiveness or final hope. Heap horrors upon the horror you have already engendered here – do things to arouse the pity of angels, to astonish the whole earth, but nothing can you do to bring greater damnation upon yourself than what, in this, you've done to us…"

He stares hard at Iago, whose body has gone limp, whose eyes are flickering closed. Othello regards him with a final, vicious stare then lets him go. Weak in the legs, Iago stumbles and falls down in a fit of coughing.

"Good God!" he sneers defiantly from the ground, making no attempt to get back on his feet. "Heaven have mercy – what kind of man are you? What's happened to you? To your mind? To your soul? God, you may as well remove me from my position too. Some wretched fool I have been who, for all his loving honesty, is now held to blame! Has the world gone mad?" he demands, throwing his head back. "Look here!" he shouts up at the sky, his tone sarcastic and disgusted. "Look here, where to be direct and open is no longer the proper thing to do. But…" He fastens his eyes on Othello. "I thank you for this most profitable lesson. Henceforward I'll be sure not to love or try helping my friends, since it does such grievous harm." In a quick movement he jumps to his feet and marches straight for the courtyard.

After a brief moment of hesitation Othello moves fast and stops Iago from leaving the garden.

"No. Stay. You do seem honest."

"I'd rather be wise," Iago snaps in reply, "for honesty too readily believes the good it seeks to do and loses all it works for in the end." He turns and starts moving again. Othello reaches out and grasps him by the arm, though not forcefully. Iago glances down at Othello's hand, then raises his eyes and regards the General's tormented face.

"As the world goes," Othello confesses, "I believe my wife is faithful, and yet something tells me she is not. I believe that you are right, and yet something tells me you are not. I must have some proof, don't you see? Her name, which was as pure and unstained as the moon above, is now besmirched and black as my own face. Be they cords or knives, poison or fire or suffocating fumes of smoke, I can't bear it. If only I could be certain!"

"I realize, sir, how consumed with passion you are. I regret that it was I who provoked you to it." He pauses and waits for Othello to look him in the eye. "You wish to be certain?"

"Wish? No, I must be!"

"And may be," Iago allows, "but the question is *how*? *How* can you be, my lord? Would you like to look on? Perhaps catch her *doing* the dreaded act itself?"

"Damnation, I'd rather die!"

Iago nods sagely. "It *would* be difficult and unpleasant to witness a spectacle like that. And damn them both," he declares, "if they let other people's eyes behold them locked in passion… But what, as I say, can be done? And how can it be done? What should I tell you about where you can find your certainty? It's impossible that you should catch them red-handed – whether they be rutting like goats, hot-coupling like monkeys, snarling like wolves peaked in their heat – and be fooled into believing what people contend: that ignorance is truly bliss. Yet, as I think about it, if an accusation drawn from circumstances sheds clear light on the truth – " He reflects for a moment. "If such a thing would allow you to be certain, I believe there could be something found."

"Give me one good reason she would be unfaithful."

"I am not comfortable doing this, my lord, but since I am so much a part of what is going on and my conscience is pricked by friendship and foolish honesty to disclose what I know, I believe I should no longer hold back." He waits for Othello to nod before continuing. "On a recent night I had occasion to share a barracks' room with Cassio, and having a raging toothache I couldn't sleep. As you may know, there are certain men so reckless and loose living that it's nothing for them to babble during their drunken sleep about personal things – Cassio is one such fellow. I heard him muttering while he slept this night, saying 'Sweet Desdemona, we must be careful, we must keep our love a secret,' and then, sir, he clutched my hand and stroked it, crying 'O sweet woman!', at which point he kissed me so hard it was as if he was yanking up kisses that grew on my lips by their roots, and then he threw his leg over my thigh, sighed some more, and kissed me again before crying out

'How cruel is fate that gave you to the Moor!'"

"This is outrageous! Outrageous!"

"No, it was only his dream, sir."

"But it showed something which had already taken place."

"A shrewd suspicion sir, yes, even though it stems from a dream, yet it may help to confirm other evidence that's less convincing."

"I'll tear her completely to pieces."

"No, not so fast, my lord. She may, up until now, have done nothing. She may still be yours after all. But tell me, have you not seen your wife with a handkerchief some times, white and sewn with strawberries upon it?"

"I gave her one like that – it was my first gift."

"I don't know about that, but such a handkerchief – I'm sure it was your wife's – I saw Cassio wipe his beard with it today."

"If that's the one – "

"If it is, or any other belonging to her, it looks bad, at least in light of other proofs."

"If only the rogue had forty thousand lives! One is not enough to take my revenge upon, now that I see how true it is. As you are my witness, Iago – I throw my foolish love away. It's gone." He bows his head, lets out a breath, casts his eyes around the garden. "Arise, black vengeance, from deepest hell –" he curses, deeply agitated. "Surrender, O worthy love, your tender heart and let it know the horrible power of tyrannous hate – " His anger builds, becomes frenzied. "Swell up, my chest, with your seething burden of venomous snakes – "

"Settle yourself, my lord," Iago pleads in a pretense of worry.

"Bloody, bloody, bloody!" Othello cries in utter wrath and falls to his knees.

"Perhaps you should be patient, sir, in case your mind should change –"

"Never, Iago! As the Black Sea's cold tide plunges ever forward, never receding, so my bloody thoughts will take their violent course and never look back – never return to the gentle straits of love until a vast and cruel revenge has purged them of their pain. Now by cold, unrelenting heaven, in due reverence for this sacred vow, I make a pledge to keep my word, so help me."

He moves to stand up but Iago rests a hand on his shoulder. "Don't get up," Iago says and kneels down beside Othello, folding his hands solemnly in prayer. "Bear witness you ever watchful powers above, you heavenly bodies that here surround us, bear witness that Iago commits the working of his mind, his hands and his heart, to righting the wrong that has been done Othello. Let him but command, and in pity I will obey and carry out whatever bloody task I must."

Moved, Othello puts his arm around Iago. "I accept your pledge not with polite thanks but whole-hearted gratitude," he says as he rises. " – And will this instant put it to the test."

Iago stands up and awaits the General's instructions.

"In three days' time," he says, "I need to hear that Cassio no longer lives."

"My friend is dead," Iago replies without hesitation. "Consider it done – as requested. But let *her* live, my lord."

"Damn her, wanton whore!" Othello erupts. "Let her go to hell! Come, let us head our separate ways. I will think over what must be done and devise a swift means of death for the fair devil." He looks squarely into Iago's eyes. "From now on you are my lieutenant."

"I am yours for ever," Iago says with calm detachment, letting Othello lead him out of the garden....

Her face part worry and part frustration, Desdemona leads Emilia down a dark corridor in a part of the castle where neither of them has ever been before.

"Where could I have lost the handkerchief, Emilia?"

Emilia halts and points Desdemona down what seems to be a main hallway. " – I have no idea, madam," she says in answer to the question.

Desdemona stops, peers warily up ahead, then offers a tentative shrug. They waste no time setting off in the new direction, Desdemona letting Emilia go first at this point, since it's her idea. "Believe me," she worries as they hurry forward, "I would rather have misplaced a purse full of gold coins if my noble Moor wasn't such a decent man and not prone to raving jealousy. Otherwise it's the kind of thing that would drive a husband to distraction."

"Is he not the jealous sort?"

"Othello? No, I think when he was young the African sun melted away such moods."

Soon the corridor opens onto a spacious area where light from an opening high above illuminates a large square in the floor whose black and white tiles, eight on all sides in game-board pattern, are spread with beautifully carved, waist-high chessmen in ebony and ivory: pawns, rooks, knights, bishops. The castle jester, in his red and green harlequin costume and bell-tipped cap, is preparing to make a move with the white queen, which is almost as tall as he is, when the two women come into the light and approach the chess board.

Desdemona starts to speak but the jester throws up his hand for silence. He studies the white queen a moment longer then slides her across the black and white squares to the other end of the board so that the white queen nudges the black knight to one side. Before taking his hands off the queen, he turns and considers the surrounding chess pieces, particularly the black king, which is now in check.

"Do you know if Cassio lies here, sir?"

"I don't know if he lies anywhere," the jester quips.

"What do you mean?"

"He's a soldier, madam. For me to say he 'lies'…" He whistles and makes a throat-slitting gesture with his hand. "…The axe. That's what I mean."

"Go on, I mean where does he reside?"

Walking over to the black king, he rushes his words. "To tell you where he resides is to tell you a lie because I can't say I know when I don't. So there."

Desdemona turns to Emilia. "Can you make anything of this?"

Suppressing a smile, she shakes her head.

"I don't know where he dwells," the jester says, his eyes intent on the chess game, "and for me to devise a dwelling and say you'll find him lying here, there or elsewhere, would mean I was dwelling upon the very lie I had devised."

Desdemona smiles patiently. "Could you inquire and have someone hereabouts inform you?"

"I could interrogate *everyone* hereabouts," he replies with an emphatic shrug, "that is, ask some questions in hopes of getting some answers."

"Could you find him for us then and ask him to come here? Tell him I have appealed to my lord Othello on his behalf and expect that all will be well."

"I could, I could," he allows pleasantly and pushes the black king safely out of check. "To do this is within the realm of capability, and therefore I shall make an attempt to do it." He whirls himself in an acrobatic jig, dances between several white pawns and trots off down a nearby corridor.

Emilia notices Othello coming toward them. "Madam," she says, alerting Desdemona. "Your husband…"

Desdemona takes up a position between the white bishop and the black rook. "I will keep after him now until he agrees to recall Cassio," she tells Emilia before turning to greet Othello.

"Good day, my lord. How do you do?" she asks tenderly.

"Well, my good lady," he says brusquely and turns aside. "How hard is this pretending! – And you, Desdemona?"

"Well, my good lord."

They meet near the center of the chessboard, Othello restless and uncomfortable. "Let me see your hand," he says.

Desdemona holds out her arm uncertainly, watches while he studies her palm.

"This hand is moist, my lady."

"It has yet to be touched by age or sorrow."

"Which means fruitful breeding and generous giving of yourself: it's also hot, hot and very moist." Desdemona looks down at the hand he has wrapped in his. "Such a hand needs time for itself, perhaps fasting and prayer, discipline and devotion, for we have here an eager young thing who gives very freely of herself. Though it is a lovely hand, and true."

"Indeed, you should say so since it was this hand which I gave away with my heart."

"A free hand. It used to be that hearts were given in marriage but now the practice is to give one's hand, not the heart."

"I'm not sure of that," she shrugs. "So, now, to your promise."

"What promise, sweet?"

"I have sent to have Cassio come and speak with you."

Othello turns his face away and coughs. "I'm bothered with a cold today. Lend me your handkerchief."

"Certainly, my lord," she says and pulls a white handkerchief from the sleeve of her dress.

Othello regards the hand but doesn't take the handkerchief. "No, the one I gave you."

"I don't have it with me at the moment."

"You don't have it…"

"Not upon me, no."

"That is a shame, for the handkerchief was given to my mother by an Egyptian woman versed in charms and spells who could read people's thoughts and foretell the future. She told my mother that as long as the handkerchief was in her possession she would never want for my father's affection and he would remain deeply in love with her. But, if she lost it or gave it away, my father would begin looking for someone else with whom he could find fulfillment. When she died she gave it to me and urged that I give it to my own wife. I did so, to you, so you could look after it and cherish it, as something precious as sight. Mislaying it or giving it away would be a loss nothing else could equal."

"Is this true?"

"Utterly. There's magic woven into the thread. A two hundred year-old seer in prophetic fury did the sewing. The worms were sacred from which the silk was drawn, and it was dyed with maiden's white, prepared from the mummified dust of virgins."

"Really, this is true?"

"Most true, therefore be very careful with it."

" – Then I wish to God I had never laid eyes on it!" Desdemona cries in frustration, stepping back so, without realizing it, she knocks down a white pawn.

"Ha, why is that?"

"Why must you speak so sharply to me?"

"Is it lost?" he presses her. "Has it gone missing?"

"For heaven's sake – "

"What's that – ?"

"It's *not* lost," she says, "but what if it were?"

"How?"

"I told you it's not lost."

"Fetch it then. Let me see it."

"I can if you wish, but I won't just now. – This is some trick to keep me from asking about Cassio."

"Fetch me the handkerchief, my patience wears thin."

"You know you can't find a more deserving man."

"The handkerchief?" He steps around the black bishop.

"First tell me what you'll do about Cassio."

"The handkerchief?"

"A man who has always set his own success by your friendship, shared danger with you – "

"The handkerchief?"

"By heaven, *you* are the one to blame – "

"God damn it!" he shouts and turns from her, kicking chess pieces out of his path as he storms across the checkered floor and away.

Shocked and confused, Desdemona can only stare after him.

"This is a jealous man," Emilia offers, to break the silence.

"I've never seen him like this. There must be something truly exceptional about the handkerchief. Of course I'm upset that I cannot find it, yet I would have thought a husband's understanding – "

"A man doesn't show his true colors for a year or two, madam," Emilia says. "They are all appetite and we are their food. They eat us hungrily to begin, and when they've had enough they belch and turn away."

A playful whistle comes from across the room. It's the jester, his arms outstretched, both index fingers pointing up at the chess piece he has managed to balance on his head. His nonsense draws a weak but grateful smile from Desdemona, but Emilia is not amused.

" – Madam, look yonder. It's Cassio and my husband…"

Marching briskly toward the women, Cassio slows up as Iago dispenses some last-minute advice.

"There is no other way, Cassio. She is the one who has to do it, but the beauty is, just like that – " he snaps his fingers, "luck will be on your side. Go on – be persistent with her."

While Cassio continues over to Desdemona, Iago hangs back, taking up a position in front of the jester, who tips his head forward and lets the chess piece fall almost to the floor before catching it. He holds it up like a telescope and pretends to peer between Iago's legs before somersaulting to one side so he can take up a better vantage point…

"Good day, dear Cassio," Desdemona smiles, "what's the news with you?"

"What I discussed with you before, madam. Again I seek your gracious help in winning back my position and returning to duty and the service of him I honor. I can't be put off any longer – if what I've done wrong means that neither my past record nor my present repentance can guarantee my future worthiness and so redeem me in the General's eyes, then I need to know that, once and for all. If it be the case that I am through, then I must abandon this course and begin looking for another career, taking whatever fortune brings my way."

"Alas, good Cassio, my pleas are not striking a harmonious note. My husband is not himself for some reason and has in fact fallen into such a frame of mind that he is unrecognizable to me at the moment. I have, so help me, spoken on your behalf to the best of my ability, incurring his great displeasure it seems by so freely speaking my mind. You must be patient at this point. I will do whatever I can – as much and even more than I would ever dare to do for myself. Let that be of some assurance."

"Is my lord angry?" Iago inquires, stepping forward to join the conversation.

"When he left us a few moments ago he was violently upset," Emilia explains.

"How could he be angry?" Iago wonders. "I've seen it when enemy cannon have blown his men to bits, a fierce barrage one time decapitating his own brother as they fought side by side – what could make him so angry hereabouts? It has to be something important," he reasons. "I will go and see, since there must be more to it if he is this incensed."

"I would be grateful for that," Desdemona says.

Bowing himself away, Iago hurries off, passing the jester who is kneeling in front of the white rook, chin resting on his arms which are folded on the castle top as he watches the others move about on the checkered floor.

" – Some matter of state business, perhaps a message from Venice," Desdemona reasons in explanation of her husband's behavior, "or possibly a conspiracy he has uncovered here in Cyprus – one of these must be keeping him from thinking clearly, which can happen if people start wrangling over small things when much greater ones are on their minds. It's the same when we hurt a hand or foot, and the rest of the body feels pain." She reflects for a moment. "No, we mustn't look upon our husbands as gods, but do our best to remember that they're only human and can't always be expected to lavish upon us the same sweet tenderness they did when we were first married. The devil take me, Emilia, for there I was, inexperienced partner that I am, taking him to task heart and soul for his unkindness, but now I see the whole thing was my own fault and I treated him unfairly."

"Pray to heaven it's matters of state then, as you suppose, and not some imaginary thought or jealous notion that he's got into his head about you."

"I hope that too, for I've never done anything with a purpose of making him jealous."

"But jealous people don't accept these simple denials, madam: they're not jealous for a reason; they're jealous because they're jealous. It's a monster that creates itself inside the mind and comes to life of its own accord."

"Heaven keep such a monster from Othello's mind, then."

"Amen, my lady."

"I will go to him. Cassio, wait here if you would. If I find him in a better mood I'll put your case forward as ever and do my utmost for you," she promises.

"I humbly thank your ladyship," Cassio says, and when Desdemona and Emilia are gone he begins pacing nervously around the black and white squares, stepping out of the way politely whenever the jester motions that he wants to place one of his chess pieces where Cassio's standing. With all the men in position, the jester indicates that Cassio is free to choose white or black. Cassio shakes his head *No*, he doesn't wish to play, but both he and the jester jump when a sarcastic female voice calls out from behind them:

"God save Cassio!"

Bianca, a local courtesan with hard, bawdy beauty, strolls toward the lieutenant, a surly pout on her red lips as she lets him get an ample eyeful of her robust cleavage.

A guilty look on his face, Cassio goes toward her. "What are you doing here – why aren't you at home?" He moves to take her hands but she sneers and bats them away.

"How are you fair Bianca? Sweet girl, I swear I was coming to see you – "

" – But I've come to see you instead. A week has gone by with no sign of Cassio. Seven days and nights have gone by. Seven times twenty-four hours have gone by, and each of those hours without Cassio more trying than…" She searches for a comparison: " – Than seven times twenty-four, times *all* the hours on the clock, and Bianca by herself left to count them one, by one, by one – "

"Forgive me, Bianca," he says, pleading with her. "I have lately been weighed down with some pressing business." Falling for his charms this time, she lets him take her hands and put them to his lips. "But I shall make up for every one of my absences…" he murmurs softly, kissing her throat, her cheeks, "by not letting anything interrupt my time with you again." He brushes his mouth across her lips, whispering "So help me!" and then with all forgiven, Bianca lets him kiss her until, moving to put her arms around him, Cassio unexpectedly steps back and produces Desdemona's white handkerchief embroidered with heart-shaped strawberry clusters. "Sweet Bianca, would you copy the work on this for me?"

Insulted, Bianca glares at the handkerchief. "Where did that come from?" She tries grabbing it but Cassio keeps it out of reach. "Of course," she says with a bitter scowl, "it's a gift from some new woman you've found. That's why you haven't been to see me, isn't it?" She turns away, crosses her arms and sulks. "Well, well. It's come to this," she says with disdain.

"Don't be ridiculous. Throw your cockeyed assumptions back at the devil who had you dream them up. Of course you're jealous because you think this is a keepsake from another mistress, but I'm telling you honestly Bianca, it's not."

"Well, whose is it?"

"I have no idea, I found it in my chamber. I like the heart-shaped strawberries and, before it's wanted back, as it surely will be, I wanted to have it copied. Take it and do it for me?"

He holds the handkerchief out. Bianca folds her arms and bites her bottom lip while she looks at the handkerchief and tries to make up her mind. Cassio gently touches it to her cheek so she can feel the softness. Without a word she snatches it from him and slips it between her breasts.

"Now leave me be," he says uneasily.

"Leave you be? Why?"

"I'm waiting for the General to meet me here, and right now it won't be to my advantage, nor do me any good to be seen in the company of a woman."

"Why not?" She presses her body against his.

"Not that I don't love you."

" – But you *don't* love me," she protests, her mouth so close he can feel the warmth of her breath on his neck. "Look," she says quietly, cosying up to him and taking his hand. "Just walk with me for a little while and tell me that one night soon we will be together again." She rubs the top of his hand against her cheek, kisses the palm, lets his fingers graze the swell of her breast as she lowers his hand and pulls him toward one of the nearby corridors.

"I only have a few minutes…"

"That's fine."

"The General will be here."

"Mm-hmm."

"But I will see you soon. I will…"

"That's good to hear: just don't forget, I'm a woman who knows her place…"

Growing steadily more furious, Othello follows as Iago leads him quickly along an upstairs corridor past tall, oil-painting portraits of governors, military figures and lofty sailing ships at anchor in Cyprus harbor.

"And what do you think?" Iago asks the General.

"What do I think?"

"Yes, if he kisses her in private."

"It doesn't matter where – there should be no kisses."

"And naked in bed with him for more than an hour, that can do no harm?"

"Naked in bed, and do no harm? Come Iago. That's worse than hypocrisy: you can seem virtuous and not be so, that's letting heaven down. But seeming to be evil yet having no harm in mind..." He leaves the thought unfinished as they reach the end of the hall and head down stairs.

"So they do nothing," Iago shrugs, "it's a forgivable mistake. But if I give my wife a handkerchief – "

"If you do, what then?"

"Why then it's hers, my lord, and being hers she may, in my opinion, give it to anyone she likes."

"She's the protector of her reputation too, can she give that away as she likes?"

"Her reputation is something others see and therefore not hers to give. It's something we imagine to be there when very often those who have it actually have it not. As for the handkerchief – "

"Good lord, I would be just as happy to forget about it! You said – and it haunts me like a grave omen – you said he had my handkerchief, didn't you?"

"I did, but what of that?"

"I'm convinced now it's not right."

"What if I told you I had seen him do you wrong, behind your back perhaps? Or heard him say – as scoundrels will do snooping about, making threats, offering bribes, or letting some broken-hearted old mistress blab on – "

"Has he said anything?"

"He has, my lord, but rest assured it's nothing that he wouldn't take back if he had to."

"What has he said?"

"Well, that he – " Iago's reluctant to say.

"That he *what*?"

"I don't know."

"What?"

"He did – "

At the bottom of the stairs, Iago turns them toward the lighted area where the jester has all his chess men in their proper places.

"What, what?" Othello demands, beside himself.

"Lie."

Soon they come to the checkered floor, the jester pondering a move nearby.

"With her?"

"With her, on her, what have you."

"Lie with her? Lie on her?" Agitation registers deeply in Othello's face as he struggles with the picture Iago has suddenly painted. "We say 'Lie on her' when we lie to her. But 'Lie with her', damn! that's repulsive to any man! – Handkerchief! She confesses. Handkerchief! He confesses, and is rewarded for his labor to be my lieutenant again?" His whole body has begun convulsing. "First to be rewarded – then to confess – I'll not think of it. Nature would not have engendered so secret a passion without human prompting." He moves about the floor trying to control the movement of his body so the others don't see him shaking. "It's not words that cause me to shudder!" he cries to Iago and the jester. "Pah! It's whispers! Smells! Kisses – is it possible? Confess – Handkerchief – O God – " But before he can finish he falls to the floor, writhing in epileptic seizure.

Iago sees the jester looking on in horror as the great General's body thrashes uncontrollably. He hurries over to say something. The jester shakes his head and points down the closest corridor, at which point Iago nods and sends the jester scurrying off, the bells on his fool's cap jingling as he goes.

"Do your worst, my medicine," Iago says with a cold smile, "your worst! This is the way pitiful fools are undone and many an innocent woman disgraced." Staring down at the floor as the fit continues, with his foot he clears black and white chess pieces out of Othello's way. He looks up at the sound of jingling bells: the jester is returning with Cassio. He drops to his knees and makes it seem as if he's been tending to Othello.

"My lord! My lord, I say, Othello! How now, Cassio – "

"What happened?"

"My lord's epilepsy. This is the second fit in as many days."

"Rub his temples," Cassio suggests and crouches beside Iago to do just that.

"No," Iago says, holding him back, "leave him alone. The fit must take its natural course, otherwise he'll start foaming at the mouth, after which there's a violent outburst."

Cassio rises and glances at the jester, who shrugs and continues to watch Othello.

"Look, he's coming to. Go elsewhere for a little while, Cassio. He'll recover straightaway. When he's gone I'd like to speak to you about something important."

A look of sympathy for his friend on the ground and Cassio departs, the jester following along when Iago signals him to leave as well.

"How is it General?" Iago asks Othello, who is awake but dazed as he peers up at his ensign. "Your head has suffered a terrible blow."

After some effort Othello manages to sit up.

"Are you mocking me?"

"Mocking you? No, not at all. I only hope you can accept what's happened as any man would."

"A cuckold is a man with horns and a beast of a man at the same time."

"There's many a beast in the populated cities then, and many a man with horns walking the streets."

Othello rubs his jaw and lets out a breath. "Has he admitted to anything?"

Iago makes a face. "Good sir, just accept it like a man, realizing every married fellow is strapped to the same yoke, bearing the same burden you are. There's millions out there who lie each night in beds that are, so to speak, no longer their own, and which they wish no one else was sharing: again, so to speak. But at least you know the truth. It's hell's malicious doing, Satan's mocking way, to have us assume a lover's faithful because she's kissing us in our own beds. No, I'd rather know, as you do, and knowing what I am, I know exactly what she is too."

"You are a wise one, Iago, that's for sure," Othello offers as he gets to his feet, Iago steadying him because he's still woozy.

"Stand over here if you would," says Iago, indicating an alcove under the staircase, "where you're out of sight but can still listen to what is said." He helps Othello across the checkered floor and over to the area beneath the stairs. "While you were in the throes of your distress – a condition most unbecoming to a man like yourself – Cassio came by. I got him out of the way and made up a good excuse for what had happened to you, and told him to return later so I could speak to him alone, which he promised to do."

Iago places the General in the shadows so he's not visible. "You stay hidden here and take note of the mocking sneers and contemptuous laughter that comes from him. For I will have him tell the story of where, how, how often, how long ago, and when next he plans to have your wife – "

Hearing this, Othello starts angrily and steps into the light. Iago takes him by the shoulders and walks him back.

"As I say, merely watch how he behaves – and stay calm, I tell you, or I'll be persuaded anger has completely consumed your manhood." He moves back toward the chess floor.

"Can you hear me?" Othello asks from the shadows. "You will be impressed with how calm I can be but – can you hear me?" He steps into the light again. "Severely calm, Iago…"

"That's to be expected, considering what you will be listening to, but remember to control yourself." He waves at Othello. "Back now, under the stairs."

Alone on the checkered floor, Iago stands up the chess pieces that have been knocked over. "Now I will question Cassio about Bianca," he murmurs to himself as he moves about the floor, "a strumpet who sells herself so she can buy food and clothes. She's infatuated with Cassio – as happens to women when they live by enticing many but who eventually find themselves enticed by one they believe will see through to the good in them. When he hears me talk about her he won't be able to resist laughing out loud – here he comes." He gives Othello a subtle signal wave, and positions himself.

Cautious while he makes sure Othello is gone, Cassio looks relieved when Iago beckons him forward to talk.

"Cassio's smiles will drive the General mad," Iago says quietly with his eyes on the approaching lieutenant, "his ignorant jealousy taking every gesture, joke and grin completely the wrong way – " He beams a friendly smile. "How goes it lieutenant?"

"Worse when you address me with the title I want so badly to recover that it nearly kills me."

"Keep working on Desdemona and you're sure to get what you're after," Iago advises and lowers his voice. "Just imagine if it were up to Bianca how quickly things would be taken care of," he laughs and winks.

"The poor wretch," Cassio says with a convivial chuckle.

"Look how he's already laughing," Othello bristles to himself in the staircase shadows…

"I never knew a woman so hopelessly in love with a man as she is with you," Iago continues with Cassio.

"Silly woman," Cassio says with a shake of his head, "I almost feel sorry for her. I think she's truly smitten – but why me?" he asks with a joking laugh.

"A half-hearted denial," Othello murmurs, "and he keeps laughing just the same…"

"But really," Iago lowers his voice again and becomes deadly serious, "what's this I hear about the two of you?"

"Now he probes for details of the affair – yes, well done Iago, well done…"

Cassio gives the ensign a questioning look.

"Why, she's spreading the word that the two of you are getting married. Is it true?"

Taken aback until he realizes this is Iago's idea of a joke, Cassio bursts out laughing: "You must be kidding!"

"The victor gloats over his conquest, does he?" Othello seethes in anger…

"Me, get married! – A paying customer? Please. A little respect if you will. I'm not that stupid – or filthy-minded," he laughs and nudges Iago in the ribs, a little too hard for the ensign's liking.

"So, so, so, so," Othello simmers, "he who laughs last – "

"Well," Iago continues, "the rumors are that you and the wench are betrothed."

"Come now, Iago," Cassio objects. "I'm a very villain if it's not true," he adds, crossing his heart and holding up his hand as though to swear on it.

"And I'm to be put into storage? Well," Othello says, staring fixedly ahead…

"This is what the little vixen's saying, is she," Cassio responds. "Convinced I'm going to marry her." He shakes his head. "She flatters herself to think so – it's not my doing I can tell you."

Iago very subtly shifts position so he's nearer to the stairs.

"He wants me to listen now – " Othello notes. "The story's going to come out…"

"She was here just now," Cassio explains. "She stalks me everywhere these days. I was down by the harbor the other morning, talking with some Venetians, when along she comes and, I swear, breaks right into the conversation and flings herself at me – "

" – Crying 'O dearest Cassio!' of course, " Othello fumes bitterly as Cassio performs a mock embrace on himself for Iago's benefit, " – that's what this wrapping of arms shows…"

"She has her hands all over," Cassio complains, "drapes herself around my neck, clinging tight while she weeps and sobs like there's no tomorrow, then she tries to drag me off – ha!" he chortles, "you should have seen her!"

"Now the part about how she plucked him off the street and took him straight to my bedroom," Othello sneers. "I see the bone here, but he's not the dog I will throw it to…"

"Well, I suppose I have no choice now but to end it," Cassio shrugs.

"Why, speak of the devil," Iago says, noticing a livid Bianca tearing toward them.

"The alley cat herself, though more sweetly scented," Cassio chuckles. "Listen, you little devil, what do you *mean* by stalking my every move?" he demands.

Her feelings hurt, she walks up and starts slapping him in the face, arms and chest – anywhere she can land a blow – the lieutenant working to dodge her surprisingly quick hands.

"Let the devil and his mother stalk you if they like!" she rails, " – what did you *mean* giving me that handkerchief just now? What a fool I was to take it – and you wanting me to copy the stitching! Ha! A likely story – that you just *happened* to find it lying in your bedroom and have *no* idea in that head of yours who could *possibly* have left it there! I'm not stupid. It's a present from one of your floozies, and you'd like me to sew another one for you – what, so you can give that one away too?" She takes out the white handkerchief and throws it in his face. "There, give it to your little tramp! Wherever you got it from, I don't care. I'm not touching it. So there!"

"What's this, my sweet Bianca, what's this?" Cassio frowns and slips his arms around her. "What's the matter?" But Bianca quickly shoves him away.

"My handkerchief!" Othello declares to himself.

"You wish to know what's the matter?" Bianca asks. "Come to supper tonight and I just might tell you," she says curtly. "Of course, if you don't, well, just forget you ever had anything to do with me." She wheels abruptly and marches off down a corridor past the jester, who sits cross-legged on the floor, waiting till the others have gone before resuming his chess game.

"After her!" Iago urges, "after her!" He hurries Cassio away from the staircase.

"I suppose if I don't she'll go shouting it through the streets…"

"Not what someone in your position can afford right now. Will you meet her for supper after all?"

"I imagine so."

Iago pushes Cassio to get a move on. "I may stop in to see you," he calls. "There's a matter we need to discuss!"

"Would you?" Cassio asks hopefully.

Iago nods and puts a finger to his lips. "Shh, say no more. Go!"

Cassio has barely hurried off to catch Bianca when Othello charges from his hiding place.

"How shall I murder him, Iago?"

"Did you see how he laughed about his escapades?"

"How could I not?"

"And did you see the handkerchief?"

"It was mine, was it not?"

"Yours, certainly. And did you hear his opinion of your wife?" Iago shakes his head in disgust. "Letting a whore have the very handkerchief she had given him."

"I would have him die a slow and painful death." Othello looks down, his mind wandering. "Such a fine woman," he says absently, "so beautiful, so sweet – "

"It's best you don't think like that, my lord," Iago says coldly.

Othello meets the ensign's eyes. "Yes. I should let her suffer and then die, and be done with her tonight. Her life is over now," he says with difficulty. "My heart has turned to stone. I touch it – " He feels his chest, "and it hurts my hand…" For a moment he is silent, unconvinced in his anger. "But the world has no sweeter being than she – she could lie with emperors and rule them like no other," he says fondly.

"That's not the way to think of her now," Iago reminds him, almost scolding.

"Perhaps not. But I can't pretend I no longer love her." He lets himself remember. "Her music, her wanting to know so much about me – she could charm thoughts from a philosopher, Iago."

"She's the worse for being able to, my lord."

"A thousand and a thousand times…" Othello says longingly, his voice trailing off. He can barely bring himself to speak. "She so loved me. I know it…"

"Perhaps too well," Iago says rancorously, although Othello is so steeped in private reverie he doesn't hear.

"This is the tragedy of it, Iago," he lets out as though grief-stricken. "The tragedy of it." He lowers his hand and lets his fingers touch the chess piece that stands before him: the white queen…

Disgusted, Iago turns away so his back is to Othello. "If you're so fond of what she's done to you," he says with biting sarcasm, "from now on let her do whatever she pleases, for if it bothers you not, it bothers no one else."

"I will tear her to pieces!" Othello erupts after a moment. "Cuckold me!"

"It's a vile thing she's done – "

"With my own lieutenant – "

"Which makes it even worse."

"Get me some poison by tonight. I'll not argue with her, in case her wiles and tender beauty render me helpless once again. Tonight, Iago."

Iago shakes his head. "Don't do it with poison. Strangle her in her bed – the very bed she contaminated."

"Good, yes. The justice of it I like. Good."

"And as for Cassio, leave him to me. You shall hear more by midnight."

"Excellent – "

Trumpets announce someone's arrival in the hall beyond the staircase. Iago and Othello promptly move into the adjacent rotunda, the echo of the musical fanfare resounding high in the domed ceiling overhead.

"It's Lodovico and a delegation from the duke," Iago says. "And look, your wife is with them."

Desdemona tries to catch Othello's eye as Lodovico and his entourage assemble before the General, who refuses to look in his wife's direction.

Lodovico salutes and presents himself. "God save you, General."

"Thanks, Lodovico, with all my heart."

"The Duke and senators of Venice greet you," he says with cordial formality, having an attendant hand him a leather portfolio with the government's coat-of-arms blazoned in gold, which he then passes to Othello.

"I welcome their orders," the General replies, holding up the portfolio solemnly, "and relish news of their wishes." He steps to a military table Iago has quickly made ready and begins going through the documents.

"And what is the news, good cousin Lodovico?" Desdemona inquires, stepping forward. Othello notices but doesn't acknowledge her.

"Very happy to see you, senator," Iago puts in quickly and bows before the emissary. "Welcome to Cyprus."

Lodovico notices in a glance that Iago now wears a lieutenant's stripes on his uniform. But when no other officer presents himself, Lodovico awkwardly offers the ensign a dignified "Thank you" and nods uncertainly to the other soldiers on Othello's staff. "How is Lieutenant Cassio?" he finally asks.

"Surviving, sir," Iago says.

"I should tell you, cousin," Desdemona explains, "there's been a falling out between him and my lord. An unfortunate quarrel really – but I'm sure your presence shall make it all well – "

"How can you be sure of that?" Othello snaps.

"My lord?" Desdemona asks, having heard him say something.

Othello covers his interjection by reading from a letter out loud. "'This you cannot fail to do, as you will – '"

Lodovico sees Desdemona's discomfort. "He didn't answer because he's busy with the papers," he says gently. But he takes her aside to speak more confidentially. "A quarrel between Cassio and your husband?" he asks uneasily.

"A severe one," she nods. "I've done everything I can to reconcile them, because of how I feel for Cassio."

"Hell and damnation!" Othello blurts out.

"My lord?" Desdemona asks again.

"Are you out of your mind?" he demands furiously, but again makes it seem as though he's questioning the contents of something he's just read.

"What, is he angry?" Desdemona wonders.

"No doubt the letters have upset him. For I believe he is being ordered back to Venice, leaving Cassio in charge here."

"To be honest, I am happy to hear it."

" 'To be honest'?" Othello says, annoyed.

"My lord?" Desdemona asks once more.

"I am happy..." Othello broods, adding quietly: "To see you've gone mad."

"Why, sweet Othello?"

He puts down the papers and moves to confront his wife.

"Devil!" he explodes, cuffing her across the face with the back of his hand.

"I did not deserve that," Desdemona protests, quickly taking a handkerchief to her bleeding nose and lips.

Aghast, Lodovico cries out: "My lord! They would not believe this in Venice, though I swore I had seen it with my own eyes. It goes too far," he declares sternly. "Apologize. She is in tears."

"To hell with it!" Othello says, coming away from the table with a document in his hand. "If her tears were teeming over the earth it would not feel a bit of moisture, for every drop would prove false. Out of my sight!"

"I will not stay if it offends you so," Desdemona says softly and makes her way toward the open staircase.

"This is a good wife – I appeal to your lordship, call her back."

Othello avoids Lodovico's eyes but goes along with his request. "Mistress!" he calls.

Part way up the stairs, Desdemona turns. "My lord?"

Lodovico gestures for her to return, and so she does.

"What would you like to do with her, my lord?" Othello demands, a tone of lurid sarcasm in his voice.

"I, my lord?" Lodovico asks, increasingly puzzled by the way Othello's carrying on.

"Yes, you said you wanted her to come back. She has come back, sir, and she can go and come yet again, and keep on coming and going if that is your pleasure. And she can cry, sir, cry with the best of them," he says raising his voice, "for as you say she's good, sir, very, very good." Hurt by the cruelty of his words, Desdemona's lips tremble and her eyes brim with tears. " – Go ahead and cry, cry for all your worth," Othello sneers then turns to Lodovico. "Now, concerning this, sir," he says, holding up the document in his hand, but as he does so his glance falls on Desdemona " – Clever show of tears," he says disdainfully.

" – I am ordered home, then?" he asks Lodovico evenly. "Get away from me," he snaps at Desdemona the next moment, "I'll send for you later. – Sir, I shall obey the command and return to Venice. – Go!" he shouts at his wife. "Be off!" He returns to the table, gathers up the remaining letters and puts them in the portfolio.

Desdemona goes back and quickly disappears upstairs, her attendants frightened and confused as they hurriedly follow.

Othello gives the portfolio to Iago and turns to Lodovico. "Cassio will take my place," he says. "Well, then, may we dine together tonight?"

Lodovico acknowledges the invitation with a nod.

"You are welcome in Cyprus, sir," Othello says and, their business concluded, moves off, his officers falling in behind the General as he goes. "No better than goats and monkeys!" he barks to himself, disgusted.

Troubled, Lodovico confronts Iago. "Is this the noble Moor whom the senate so admires for his excellence and capability? The man renowned for never losing his head nor his self-control?"

"He is much changed, I know," Iago offers.

"Is he all right, I mean in his mind?"

Iago shrugs. "He is what he is, sir. I can't pass an opinion on what that might be. If what he might be, he isn't, I would wish, so help me, he was."

Lodovico looks away while considering the remark.

"But hitting his wife…"

"I know. That wasn't right, in the least. Yet I fear this blow was the worst he ever gave."

"Does he make a habit of this?" Lodovico demands, raising his eyebrows. "Or have the letters somehow upset him and brought this on?"

"If it is a habit or it isn't," Iago replies, "I'm not free to speak about things I've witnessed or experienced. You'll have to see for yourself, and let his behavior determine your own thoughts rather than have me be the one to inform you. I suggest you go after him now and see how he conducts himself."

"I regret that I may have been mistaken about him," Lodovico says, ruefully shaking his head as he turns and heads out of the rotunda.

Standing by himself a moment, Iago smiles when he notices the jester timidly approaching, Desdemona's white handkerchief in hand….

His black military cape flowing out behind him, Othello strides purposefully down the castle hall, oblivious to the stares of soldiers and household staff who step out of his way as he passes, Emilia doing her best to keep up with him.

"You haven't seen anything, then?"

"No, nor heard anything or ever suspected anything."

"Yet you've seen Cassio and…she together."

"But I saw no harm in that, and I heard every word that passed between them."

"There was no whispering, about secret things?"

"None, my lord."

"You were never asked to leave while they talked?"

"Never."

"To fetch something for her?"

"Never," she repeats.

"That is what I find strange."

"I would pledge all I have that she is faithful, my lord. I would swear my life on it. If you think otherwise, put such notions out of your mind, I tell you, for they're untrue and, moreover, they're unworthy of you – if some despicable wretch has led you to think this way, may he reap heaven's condemnation, for if she is not chaste, loyal and true, then husbands everywhere have reason to worry that the purest among their wives are deserving of nothing but the filthiest slander."

Leaving Emilia's comment unanswered, he stops at the open door of a prayer chapel.

"Go and tell her I want to see her," he snaps. "Now."

His surliness making her fearful, Emilia promptly bows and leaves to find Desdemona.

Othello enters the chapel, pale light from above filling the middle of the room. Pensive and brooding, he walks down the narrow aisle between pews toward the altar, where light from votive candles flickers in the polished surface of the gold cross, scripture pedestal and burnished candlesticks.

"What she tells me is believable enough, but it's the banter of brothels. She would never say what goes on behind closed doors. She's a deceptive one, good at keeping things to herself, yet no matter how outrageous her secret, she has no trouble putting on a penitent face and bowing her head when it's time for prayer. I've seen her do that – " He glances up to see Emilia and Desdemona slipping quietly into the chapel.

"What is it you wish, my lord?"

"Come over here, my sweetness."

Emilia remaining near the door, Desdemona advances to join Othello near the altar.

He pauses before turning to her.

"What is your pleasure?" she asks to break the silence.

"Look me in the eye."

She does. "What is this horrible imagining that haunts you, my lord?"

He casts a sharp glance at Emilia, who is watching anxiously.

"Back to work, Madam," he shouts bitterly. "Shut the door and let your customer alone so he can have the privacy he's paid for. Cough or make noise if anyone comes. Get selling your wares, Madam. Go!" he shouts again, waving her to leave.

Confused and disconcerted, Emilia reluctantly goes out and closes the door behind her.

"What would you have me know, my lord?" she demands, kneeling before him. "I understand the fury in your words, but not the words themselves."

"Because of what you are," he says harshly.

"I am your *wife*, my lord, your true and loyal wife."

He points her to the altar. "Then swear on it here and damn yourself," he tells her, "for as one of heaven's own, the devil won't take you until you do: so be damned above as you are below and swear you are faithful to me."

"Heaven knows I am."

"Heaven knows you are false as they come."

"To whom, my lord? With whom? How am I false?"

"Oh Desdemon, away, away, away!" he cries, and, turning his head aside, begins to sob.

"Alas, what sorrow this is," Desdemona says gently. She tries to see his face but he keeps his back to her. "Why do you weep, my lord? Am I then the cause of these sad tears? If you believe my father had a hand in recalling you to Venice, lay not the blame before me: if you have lost him, I have lost him too." Without thinking, she draws a handkerchief from her sleeve and offers it to him. He glares at it sullenly for a moment before looking away, wiping his eyes with the back of his hand.

"If heaven had seen fit to test me with afflictions, rained all manner of sores and shames on my bare head, cast me into dire poverty and my utmost dreams into captivity, I would still have found a drop of hope somewhere in this soul to bear my suffering. – But alas, to have fixed me under the sun, like a dial face for the scornful hand of time to point his slowly moving shadow at…though I could bear that too and bear it well, very well. Yet here in my heart," he says sadly, "where I have stored my love for you – either to live with it or die without it – the spring from which my very life flows or else dries up – to have it stopped so it's but a stagnant pool where foul toads grovel and breed…" His face showing no expression, he looks down at his left hand.

Desdemona watches in disbelief as he removes his wedding ring and sets it on the altar.

"Turn your complexion there," he says and lifts his eyes to the fresco paintings of winged angel infants on the walls around the altar. "Look, you young and rose-lipped cherubim. Look here…" He fastens his eyes on the ring. "…No more."

The next moment he has turned and started for the door.

Desdemona, snatching up the ring, pursues him. "I wish my lord would think me virtuous still!"

"I wish it too!"

"My lord!" she cries, clutching at his arms to keep him from leaving.

"You are a weed!" he says fiercely. "Who seemed herself so lovely, fair, and smelled so sweet my being could never stop the ache of wanting her – but now I wish she had never been born!"

"What sin in my ignorance have I committed?" she demands, rushing ahead and turning to block the aisle.

Othello halts in front of her.

"Was this fair page," he says, taking in her face and body, "and was this beautiful book made to have 'whore' written upon it? You well know what you have 'committed.'

"Committed?" he laughs scornfully. "No more than a common whore – my face would burn in shame were I to speak of your deeds. Don't talk to me of 'committed.' Heaven holds its nose over what you've 'committed', the moon winks at what you've 'committed,' the rude wind that happily kisses all it meets has hidden itself in a deep earth cave so it need not hear what you've 'committed.' No more about 'committed' you degenerate filth – "

"You do me wrong!" she protests.

He tries to step around her but she stands in his way.

"Are you not a harlot?"

He moves to the other side but again she prevents him from leaving.

"No, as I am a Christian!"

Othello shifts to the other side but she quickly blocks the way.

"If to keep this body belonging to my lord from any hated, foul, unlawful touch is not to be a harlot, I am not one!"

"You deny it? You say you're not a whore?"

"No, God save me!"

He shakes his head, incredulous. "Is it possible?"

"O Heaven forgive us – " she pleads, tears streaming down her face as she looks to find his hand and put the wedding ring back on his finger.

Livid, Othello grips her by the wrists so hard she drops the ring and cries out in pain.

"Mercy on you then – I mistook you for that cunning whore of Venice who married Othello!" he roars in her face, shaking her madly before he throws her out of his way with such force she bangs her head on one of the pews as she falls to the floor. Not done, he leans over her collapsed body. "You, mistress, with your harlot's chamber opposite Saint Peter – turning your trade at the very gates of hell – you, you, yes you!"

Reaching the door, Othello storms past a startled Emilia, who has come in during the commotion. "We have finished here," he says bluntly, tossing her a small pouch. "There's money for your fee, lady. Lock up when you're done," he says going out the door, but quickly steps back in. "And you will keep quiet about this," he warns, turns fast, and is gone.

"Alas, what does he mean?" Emilia worries, and grows alarmed when she spots Desdemona lying on the chapel floor between pews. "Madam!" she calls and rushes over. "Are you all right?" She helps Desdemona onto a seat in the pew. "Are you hurt, madam?"

Desdemona only stares at the gold wedding ring in her hand, shaking her head absently, as if in a trance.

Concerned, Emilia takes out her handkerchief and dabs the blood coming from the cut in Desdemona's forehead. "How are you, my good lady?"

"I am numb, Emilia," Desdemona replies without looking up from the ring.

"Goodness, madam, what's wrong with my lord?"

"With whom?"

"Why, with my lord, madam."

"Who is your lord?"

"He that is yours, my lady."

Desdemona sits in silence for a moment. "I have none. Do not talk to me, Emilia. I cannot cry and have no answers, except what might be said with tears." She pauses, her eyes cast down. "I would like you to put my wedding sheets on my bed tonight. Please remember to do that, and…" She turns to Emilia. "Ask your husband to come here at once."

"My husband?"

Desdemona nods.

"But madam – " Emilia protests, applying her handkerchief to Desdemona's forehead again.

"Please," Desdemona objects, and pulls Emilia's hand away.

Emilia lets out a frustrated breath, gets up and heads reluctantly for the chapel door. "This is most strange," she says, upset, and closes the door behind her as she departs.

Alone, Desdemona murmurs something, however no sound comes from her lips. She takes in her chapel surroundings, hands folded in her lap, nervously slipping Othello's wedding ring on her finger, then off...

"No!" she says finally, as if in response to Emilia's previous comment, "it's *fitting* he should treat me so, very fitting. How I must have behaved for him to attach the least blame to my greatest fault..."

For some time she gazes at the paintings of children with angel wings on the walls above the altar, so immersed in her own thoughts that she only notices Emilia has come back with Iago when he sits down in the pew beside her and asks: "What can I do to help, madam?"

"I cannot tell. Those who teach young children do so with patience and gentle scolding when it's called for, do they not? He might have done the same with me," she says softly, "for heaven knows I am but a child and must be scolded in like fashion."

Iago glances at Emilia, who motions for him to say something.

"What's the matter, my lady?" he inquires with what appears to be genuine concern.

"My lord has accused her of being but a whore," Emilia puts in bluntly, "and hurled such spiteful and vicious words at her which none but the coldest hearts could be expected to bear."

"Am I one, Iago?"

"One what, fair lady?"

"One of those Emilia said my lord did say I was."

"He called her 'whore.'" Emilia says the word for Desdemona. "Even a beggar in drunken temper would not have used that on his slut."

"But, why would he do so?" Iago wonders, frowning.

"I don't know," Desdemona says, her voice shaking, "though I can say I am no such thing," she protests, and begins to cry.

Iago slides closer in the pew and places a consoling arm around her shoulder. "Now now, madam, don't cry," he offers in commiseration, "there's no need for tears." He pats her shoulder affectionately, taking one of her hands and holding it comfortingly in his own. "Alas that it should come to this," he says sadly, letting his head stray close so that, with his back to Emilia, he can catch a brief scent of Desdemona's hair.

"Did she forsake so many noble matches," Emilia demands in righteous indignation, "defy her father, leave her country and her friends – just to have herself called a *whore*?" Desdemona starts at the sound of the word. "It's enough to bring anyone to tears!"

"It is my cross to bear, Emilia."

"Yet it should not be," Iago objects. "What's come over him that he would speak this way?"

"Heaven only knows," Desdemona shrugs, withdrawing her hand from Iago's to wipe tears from her eyes, letting out a hurt sigh as she does do.

"I know what has happened," Emilia says, speaking boldly, "a worthless, conniving rogue – some devious, cheating scoundrel – has made this scheme to gain favor with his betters or garner some promotion."

"Nonsense," Iago says with conviction, "there's no one who would stoop to such behavior, it's impossible."

"If there were such a man, heaven have mercy on him," Desdemona says and gets to her feet. She steps past Iago, enters the aisle and walks toward the altar.

"Let the noose have mercy!" Emilia rails. "Hell gnaw his bones!" She turns to Iago while Desdemona gazes up at the wall paintings that depict lambs and angels frisking around graceful shepherds in green fields with colorful birds sitting on their shoulders, hovering overhead. "How dare he call her whore? Who has she been with? Where, and when, and in what circumstance? And what's his proof when the likelihood is none at all? The Moor's been the victim of some despicable knave, I tell you, some notorious, groveling knave, some sick and bitter soul." The vehemence in her voice resounds in the small chapel. "I would to heaven we knew so that every good person could take up the whip and lash the villain naked from east to west throughout the world!"

"Pipe down, woman," Iago says sharply.

"Why?" she asks, her voice verging on sarcasm, "wasn't it such a rare fellow who brought out the ugliness in you when he made you suspect the Moor and me?"

"You are a fool, hush up!" Iago snaps.

" – Good Iago," Desdemona says, studying a tall, burning candle in one of several brightly polished gold candlesticks on the altar, "what shall I do to win back my lord?"

She takes up the candlestick and brings it close to her face so the flame is right in front of her eyes. "Good friend, go to him, for by this heavenly light I know not how I lost him." She watches the flame for another moment and then sets the candle back on the altar and goes down on her knees, folding her hands in prayer. "Here I kneel. If I ever trespassed against his love in thought, word or deed, or if my eyes, my ears or any other sense have taken delight in someone other than him, or if I do not still, always did and always will – though he leave me destitute and divorced – love him dearly, may I never know a single moment's comfort until the day I die. The absence of his love may hurt, and it may destroy me, but it will never weaken my love for him. I cannot easily say 'whore': I abhor the very sound of the word. I could not commit those acts that would earn me such a title, not for all the vanity and adulation in the world."

In the silence that follows, Iago throws Emilia a menacing glare that sends her to the chapel door. He then moves down the aisle toward Desdemona. "You mustn't worry, madam," he offers, "it's merely a passing mood. The business of the state has proven frustrating and he has taken out his temper on you."

"If it were only that – "

"But it is, madam, I assure you – "

A trumpet fanfare sounds in the corridor outside the chapel.

"They're summoning us to supper," Iago explains. "The messengers from Venice will be waiting."

He motions for her to precede him, but she slips her arm through his. They walk down the aisle together, Iago unable to suppress a self-satisfied smirk as he approaches Emilia.

Outside the chapel, Desdemona waits until Emilia has closed the chapel door. She withdraws her arm from Iago's, smiling appreciatively despite the worry that still shows in her face.

"Go into dinner, my lady. And no more crying," he says gently, "all things shall be well."

His wife and Desdemona heading downstairs, Iago turns and starts along the upstairs hall, only to see a man's head pop out from behind a pillar.

"Ah, Roderigo…"

"I don't feel you are playing fair with me," Roderigo declares as he steps out from behind the pillar, blocking Iago's way when the ensign-turned-lieutenant tries to keep on walking.

Having no choice, Iago halts and crosses his arms. "Why do you say that?"

Roderigo appears to mean business. He takes a breath and then holds forth, speaking quickly and nervously. "Every day you seem to brush me off with one kind of trick or another, to the point that it seems to me you're actually working to foil every chance I have for meeting Desdemona, rather than endeavoring to provide me with opportunities to have my hopes realized, and this after all I've been through. I will *not* stand for it any longer, nor will I just quietly go away after what I've foolishly let you hoodwink me into believing." Relieved, he lets out a breath as if to say "so there."

Nonplussed, Iago lets him settle down, then looks him in the eye. "Will you give me a moment to explain?"

"For goodness sake, I've listened to enough explanations already. What you say never goes hand in hand with what you do."

"Hand in hand?"

"Our actions speak louder than our words, Iago."

"Indeed, they do."

"Well then," Roderigo says with finality and crosses his arms.

"But you've leveled a most unfair accusation at me, Roderigo."

"Not at all. It's the truth and you know it. I've squandered all my money because of you. The jewels you took from me as a gift to Desdemona, even at half their value, would be enough to have the most devout religionist abandon his faith on the spot if they were put into his hands. You told me they impressed her, and led me to believe that my investment was going to bring rapid and rewarding results, yet I have seen nothing."

"All right," Iago concedes the point. "Very well – "

"'All right,' 'very well'! It is *not* all right, man, nor is it very well. As far as I'm concerned it's contemptible what you've done to me and so I find myself feeling I have been given the shabbiest treatment and, moreover, I believe I have been utterly cheated."

"All right, then," Iago shrugs and begins walking away as though their discussion is over.

"I tell you it is *not* all right!" Roderigo calls after him. "I will present myself to Desdemona and demand to know why she has spurned me," he declares adamantly, his voice echoing in the wide, empty hall. Iago puts an insistent finger to his lips and hurries back to Roderigo. "If she agrees to give back my jewels I will forego my suit and apologize for ever making inappropriate overtures. If she doesn't agree, you can be sure that won't be the end of it, for I shall come after you, Iago, for full repayment."

"Very well," Iago tells him agreeably, "now you've had your say."

"Yes, so that you know what I have every intention of doing."

Iago beams at Roderigo, impressed. "Why, now that I see there's some fight in you, sir, from now on I'll maintain a much better opinion of you than I ever have before." "Give me your hand." Roderigo does so and Iago shakes it heartily. "You're right to take exception," Iago admits, " – though I can swear in all honesty to have been perfectly straightforward with you in this business."

"Well it certainly hasn't appeared that way," Roderigo pouts.

"I agree it hasn't," Iago nods, "and I think I can say your suspicions are not without foundation. But, Roderigo, since you have that in you which I now have greater reason than ever before to believe you *do* – by which I mean determination, character, and courage – there's an opportunity for you to show it here tonight."

"An opportunity…" Roderigo says warily.

"Yes. And if by tomorrow evening you are not enjoying yourself with the lovely Desdemona, let me die a slow, painful death for, in the end, having let you down."

"Well," Roderigo mutters, taken aback by the solemnity of Iago's affirmation. "What would this involve?"

Iago glances around to make sure they're alone. He puts an arm over Roderigo's shoulder, leans in close and lowers his voice. "An official delegation has arrived from Venice to relieve the General of his command and have Cassio take his place."

"Is this true?"

Iago nods and crosses his heart.

"Why then, Othello and Desdemona will be returning to Venice."

"Oh no," Iago says, "he heads off to Mauritania, his African homeland, and the fair Desdemona will accompany him there." He pauses for the expected look of alarm to enter Roderigo's face. "Unless his stay here in Cyprus is prolonged by an accident, let us say – and what could be more convenient in that regard than something which would remove Cassio."

Roderigo eyes Iago with suspicion.

"What do you mean 'remove' him?"

Iago puts out his bottom lip and shrugs. "Why, something that would prevent him from taking Othello's place: say a harsh blow to the head…"

Roderigo clears his throat gravely. "And you would have me be the one to…"

"Yes, that is if you wanted to receive the benefit that is rightly yours." He waits before continuing. "He'll be having supper tonight with Bianca, a local prostitute, and I will be meeting him there. He hasn't yet heard that his fortunes are about to take a turn for the better. If you were to watch and follow him to her street – I will arrange for him to arrive between twelve and one – you would have a free hand to kill him. I will be nearby to back you up, and between us we can finish him off." Roderigo listens in amazement as Iago lays out his cold-blooded plan. "I'll show you that it's quite necessary for him to die, and when I have, you'll feel called upon to be the one to do it. It's about time for supper, the night is going to waste: we should get a move on."

"I will need to hear more about why we're doing this."

"You shall, Roderigo, you shall…."

4.3

At the end of the evening, Othello walks Lodovico into the castle's main foyer, Desdemona between her husband and the Venetian dignitary, Emilia and an entourage of attendants not far behind. They stop near the castle entrance and when a servant appears with Lodovico's cloak, Othello helps him put it on.

"No need to trouble yourself further, sir, I can find my way." the Venetian insists

"But a walk would do me good, sir, if it's all the same to you."

Lodovico smiles graciously and shrugs, accepts his fine wooden walking stick from the servant and turns to Desdemona. "Madam, good night to you." She extends a hand for him to kiss and he does so. About Othello's age, he is a good-looking and stylish gentleman with impeccable manners. "I humbly thank your ladyship for a fine evening."

"Your honor is most welcome."

"Are we ready then?" Othello asks, slipping on his black leather gloves. "Oh, Desdemona – "

"My lord?"

"You can head off to bed now. I will be back shortly. And dismiss your woman there for the night," he says with a curt nod toward Emilia. "See to it now."

"I will my lord," Desdemona says and starts for the grand staircase, Emilia at her side after waving the other attendants to fall in behind.

"How is he now?" Emilia inquires, gathering the folds of her dress as she and Desdemona mount the stairs. "He seems calmer than he did."

"He says he will return soon and has ordered me off to bed. He told me to dismiss you for the night."

"Dismiss me?"

"That's what he said."

Torches burning in the upstairs atrium, Emilia dismisses Desdemona's other attendants and catches up to Desdemona as she moves briskly down the corridor. They pass a number of closed doors before arriving at Desdemona's bedchamber, where Emilia opens up and they go in.

"So, good Emilia, help me with my night things and then it will be adieu. We mustn't upset him now."

"Of course," Emilia replies, but there's something bothering her as she moves about the room. "I wish you had never laid eyes on him!" she blurts out finally.

Sitting on the edge of her four-poster canopy bed, Desdemona slips off her shoes. "But I cannot feel that way," she explains, "my love for him has become so strong that even his harshness, his reprimands, his troubling frowns – unpin my hair if you would – I find attractive and charming."

Worried that she has spoken out of turn, Emilia sits on the edge of the bed and has Desdemona turn around. She removes various pins, placing each one between her lips until she's through and lets out the gorgeous blond tresses of Desdemona's hair. She plucks the pins from her mouth and puts them in a small, colorfully decorated box Desdemona holds out. "I've made the bed up with those sheets you asked for," she says.

"It's all the same I suppose…" Desdemona's mind seems to be elsewhere.

Emilia goes over to the dressing table and picks up two brushes and a comb. She returns to the bedside and starts brushing Desdemona's hair. The two women sit quietly for several moments, Desdemona humming a song to herself until finally she comes out with: "The mind is a strange thing, Emilia, don't you think?"

Emilia gives her a look. "What do you mean?"

"Well, I was thinking, if I were to die before you, you could bury me in one of these, my wedding sheets."

"Come, come, what are you talking about?" Emilia protests.

Desdemona resumes humming for a short moment before answering. "When I was a girl, my mother had a maid named Barbary. She fell in love with a man, however he went mad suddenly and left her. According to my mother she began to sing ever afterward a song about 'the willow', it was an ancient air I was told, but she felt it expressed what had happened to her and she died singing it. I can't get the song out of my head tonight for some reason. It's all I can do not to hang my head and sing it the way poor Barbary used to."

After a short silence, during which she continues brushing

Desdemona's hair, Emilia says: "This Lodovico is quite the gentleman, is he not? A very handsome man."

"He is that," Desdemona agrees.

"I know a lady in Venice who would have walked barefoot through the desert for a taste of his lips." She leans to one side, looking for Desdemona's reaction.

But Desdemona gets up, crosses the room and as she goes behind her dressing screen begins singing: "*The poor girl sat sighing by a sycamore tree, sing all a green willow. Her hand on her bosom, her head on her knee, sing willow, willow-willow. The fresh streams ran by her and murmured her moans, sing willow, willow-willow: her sad tears fell from her and softened the stones, sing willow, willow-willow.*" She drapes the clothes she's taking off over the top of the screen. "You can put these away," she calls to Emilia. "*Willow, willow-willow –* "

"Shall I fetch your nightgown?"

"Please. But we had better hurry: he could be here any minute." She takes the nightgown behind the screen. "*Sing all a green willow I'll make it my garland. Let nobody blame him, his scorn I don't mind –* No, that's not next – " The door suddenly rattles. "Is someone there?"

"It's only the wind, my lady," Emilia says and puts Desdemona's things away.

"*I called my love 'false love', but what said he then? Sing willow, willow-willow. 'If I court more women, you can sleep with more men.'*" She comes from behind the screen wearing her nightgown. "I suppose you had better go," she says and takes Emilia's hands. "Good night." She kisses Emilia on both cheeks, walks over to her dressing table and sits down. "My eyes itch now." She goes close and looks at herself in the round, gilt-framed mirror attached to her table. "Does that mean tears are coming on?"

"It might and it might not," Emilia says, coming over.

"I have heard people say so. Oh these men, these men! Tell me, Emilia," she says innocently, "do you in all honesty think there are women who go behind their husbands' backs and take lovers?"

"There are some who do, no question."

Desdemona looks at Emilia in the mirror. "Would you ever do that for anything in the world?"

"Why, wouldn't you?"

"No, by heaven's light I would not."

"Nor would I by heaven's light, but I could do it just as well in the dark," Emilia says and smiles mischievously.

"But would you do it for anything in the world?" Desdemona asks again.

Emilia considers. "The world's a huge place: there would be some price I'd take for such a small vice."

"Truly I don't think I ever would."

"In truth I think I would, and stop when I'd had enough. Mind you, I wouldn't do it merely for the tokens of love, nor measures of silk, fine clothes, or hats or precious gifts. But for anything in the world as you put it? More's the pity I'm sure, but who wouldn't cuckhold her husband to make him a monarch? I would risk going to hell for that."

"The devil take me if I could ever wrong my husband, for anything in the world."

"Well my lady, the wrong is but a wrong as far as the world goes. If you're given the world in exchange for doing such a thing, it's a wrong in your own world, and thus you could easily say it was right."

"I don't see how there could be such a woman."

"There are dozens, and so many more also that they could populate the world they were playing for. But I believe it is a husband's fault if his wife strays. What if he goes slack in his loving duties and puts what is rightfully yours in another woman's lap? Or breaks out in fits of jealousy and has your movements watched? Or what if he hits you, or cuts down on what he once enjoyed giving you, merely out of spite? Why, we feel resentment as sure as they do: and though we have some sympathy, we can also want revenge. We should let our husbands know that wives have their needs as well. We see and smell, and have a taste for the sweet and sour in life as our husbands do. What is it that they *do* when they exchange us for someone else? Is it for fun? I think so. Is it for new passion? I think it is. Is it a flaw in their character that turns them away from us? It is partly that too. But don't we have passions? Don't we desire fun, and are there not flaws in us as there are in men? Either have them show us more respect or else let them know, the wrongs we do, their wrongs have taught us so."

4.3

Thinking about what has just been said, Desdemona gets up from her dressing table and kisses Emilia on the cheek. "Good night, Emilia, good night," she says tenderly. "God keep me from learning wrong through what you've said – let me better myself by virtuous ways instead."

A knock thunders at the door. The women look to each other and, while exchanging uneasy stares, the knock comes again, even louder….

In the dark streets of Cyprus, not far from the harbor, Iago and Roderigo stay hidden against the side of a building until several loud, drunken soldiers have ambled past, shouting and belching, their bawdy women laughing and shrieking playfully while the men grope and fondle them. When all is quiet, Iago peeks into the street and, satisfied that the coast is clear, takes Roderigo by the arm and hustles him past several closed shops. In front of a fruit vendor's, he halts and surveys the surrounding area. It's a dark night anyway, but beside this particular shop it's pitch black, Iago and Roderigo barely able to see one another.

"This is good," Iago says, "stand just behind the fruit stall. Here." He has the hapless Roderigo get in position. "He'll be here any minute now."

Roderigo straightens his hat, pulls his gloves tight, and adjusts the sword belt around his waist. He's extremely nervous, wringing his hands together and biting his lips.

"Take out your sword," Iago tells him, "and remember, drive it home straightaway." Roderigo appears not to be listening: he fiddles with the collar of his shirt so that it sits right.

There's a sound of footsteps in the darkness farther down the street. Roderigo panics and starts backing away.

Taking him by the elbow, Iago returns him to the fruit stall. "Be quick remember, quick," is his advice to Roderigo. "Straight at him. And don't be afraid. It makes us or breaks us, after all, so keep to your purpose."

"Be right here," Roderigo pleads.

Iago takes out his dagger and presses the shiny, silver point against Roderigo's cheek.

"Don't worry. Now, get in position." He glances forward – the approaching footsteps are closer, and they belong to a man. Iago retreats to the alley beside the building, leaving Roderigo on his own, blinking nervously and chattering to himself.

"I have no real desire to do this deed, and yet he gave many satisfactory reasons why." Roderigo considers. "He's just one man. I take out my sword, and he dies!" He smiles weakly, only slightly buoyed up by his own words.

Iago, a pleased smile on his face as he waits for the attack to take place, leans against the building wall, balancing the point of his dagger on the tip of his tongue for a moment before letting the knife fall, catching it by the handle on its way down.

"I've fanned the sparks of this my careful fire so it begins to blaze, this angry twig about to burn for his dim ways. As to whether he kills Cassio or Cassio him, or they kill each other, every outcome means my gain. If Roderigo lives, he'll require me to return the fortune in gold and jewels I tricked from him as gifts to Desdemona: I can't have that. If Cassio survives, he has a life of easy beauty and reward which I despise. And besides, the Moor could reveal to him all I've done – which leaves me in much danger. No, he has to die. Let it be so – " He breaks off and listens to something in the street. "I hear him coming…"

Roderigo squints to see the shadow of a man nearing. "I know his walk – I'm sure this is he." At the last minute he pulls his sword from its metal sheath.

Iago winces, fearing the sound will give them away, but Cassio keeps walking.

"Die you villain!" Roderigo shouts and lunges straight at Cassio's head. His forearm up quickly, the lieutenant deftly shields himself from the blow and has his sword out instantly. "That thrust would have been my undoing, indeed, if it weren't that my coat is better than you had counted on, sir: let's see about the one you're wearing!" He rattles the sword Roderigo is now holding with two hands, swats it away and then drives his blade into Roderigo's chest.

"Ah!" he cries, "I've been slain." Blood flows over his white, ruffle-collar shirt; he teeters for a minute – staring at Cassio's sword sticking in his body – then drops to his knees and the next moment is sprawled on the cobble stones.

Moving fast, Cassio leans down to retrieve his weapon but Iago has come up from behind. They scuffle and fight, Iago missing with his dagger so it stabs Cassio in the thigh.

He cries out in pain, turning to see who's there – but Iago kicks him in the wounded leg with such force Cassio's knee buckles and he goes down. "Help! Someone! Murder here! Murder!!" He gets up on his good knee and strains his eyes to see through the darkness. All is quiet except for the sound of his own breathing. "Help here! Someone!" he calls.

But the only one who can hear him is Othello, who is rushing up the other side of the street—

"That's Cassio's voice. Iago is good to his word."

"Villain that I am," Roderigo moans quietly. "Villain…"

"It was true…" Othello murmurs to himself as he slows to see where he is going.

Knowing that someone is there, Cassio starts shouting. "Help here! Help! Bring a light! Fetch a doctor!"

"It is he," Othello says, gloating. "O good Iago, so honest and just a man, who was right in sensing your friend's wrong! You've shown me what I wanted to see. Whore!" he says, as if talking to Desdemona, "your dear one lies dead and your own end draws near. I am coming for you, those charms your eyes from my heart have disappeared – your bed, lust-stained, shall with lust's blood now be smeared…"

"Help, over here! Night guards! Anyone! Murder, I say!"

Cassio's shouts ring in the dark night air until Lodovico and Gratiano, with torches, enter the street not far away.

"Something's wrong – someone's in trouble," Gratiano says.

"Help me!" Cassio pleads, hearing their voices.

"Who's there?" Lodovico calls.

"O, wretched villain that I am," Roderigo groans, his white shirt now wet with blood.

"There are two or three of them – but it's so dark," Gratiano warns " – they could be luring us closer, it could be dangerous to do anything on our own. We should get help – "

"Is nobody there? Shall I bleed to death then?" Roderigo cries out in despair.

Meanwhile another torch flame has appeared in the darkness, on the move toward Lodovico and Gratiano.

"Hello?" Lodovico calls out.

Gratiano holds his torch away from his body and strains his eyes to see.

"Someone in his shirtsleeves, and he's armed…"

"Who's over there?" Iago demands. "Whose voice is shouting murder?"

"We don't know!" Lodovico answers.

"Did you not hear a cry for help?" Iago asks.

"Over here! Here!" Cassio calls out. "For God's sake help me!"

"What's wrong?" Iago responds.

"If I'm not mistaken," Gratiano says to Lodovico, "that one is Othello's ensign."

"True enough," Lodovico agrees, "a courageous fellow to be – "

"You over there!" Iago calls. "Who are you? What are you shouting about?"

"Iago? It's Cassio. I'm badly hurt, brought down by thieves. Give me a hand."

Running up, Iago goes to Cassio's side. "Oh no – lieutenant! What villains have done this?"

"I think one of them is still hereabouts, wounded so he can't get away."

"Contemptible cowards!" Iago says and makes a show of searching the immediate vicinity. He glances at the two torches coming nearer. "You over there! Come and give me some help."

"Oh please, help me here…" Roderigo pleads in an anguished voice.

"That's one of them!" Cassio shouts to Iago, who has located Roderigo.

"You murdering fiend!" he yells. "You foul villain!" And immediately thrusts his sword into Roderigo.

"Damned Iago!" Roderigo says hoarsely as he sees in the light from Iago's torch who it is. "Inhuman dog!"

Iago plunges his sword once again and twists it until Roderigo is no longer moving.

"Kill men in the dark, would you!" he then rages in disgust, for Cassio's benefit. "Where are the rest of these bloody thieves for me to deal with! Why is there no help? Ho there! Murder, murder!"

Gratiano motions to Lodovico, they take out their swords and close in cautiously.

"Who are you?" Iago shouts menacingly, his sword up and ready to defend against attack. "Are you for good or evil?"

"See for yourself."

"Signior Lodovico?"

"He, sir."

"I beg your pardon, sir. Cassio here's been attacked by thieves."

"Cassio?" Gratiano asks, concerned.

In answer, Iago leads the others over to Cassio, who's sitting up but wincing from the pain of his bleeding wound.

"How is it my brother?" Iago asks, sheathing his sword, passing his torch to Lodovico and kneeling down.

"My leg feels as if it's been cut in two," replies.

"Marry, let's hope not! Hold your lights closer gentlemen, I'll bandage the leg." Though it's a cool night, he tears off the sleeve and one entire side of his shirt, with which he begins to wrap Cassio's thigh.

Out searching for Cassio because he failed to meet up with her, Bianca hurries through the darkness toward the three burning torches. "What's happened? Whose voice is that calling for help?"

In a moment she can make out Cassio lying on the ground, his face and clothes covered in blood. She falls to her knees, throws her arms around his neck and smothers him with kisses. "My dearest Cassio! My sweet Cassio! Cassio," she kisses him, "Cassio," again, "Cassio," and again.

Iago grabs her arm and pulls her away so he can work. "Enough, strumpet." He concentrates on bandaging the wound. "Do you have any idea who could have done something like this, lieutenant?"

Ghostly pale, Cassio can only shake his head.

"I am sorry to see you like this," Gratiano says, visibly upset. "I had been looking everywhere for you." He crouches down, takes Cassio's hand and kisses it.

Cassio's eyes blink open briefly. "Gratiano…?"

Iago slaps Gratiano in the arm. "Lend me your belt, sir," he barks. " – Quickly." Gratiano undoes his belt and hands it to Iago. "Now if only we had a stretcher – "

"He's fainting!" Bianca cries, " – oh Cassio, Cassio!"

Finishing the bandage, Iago makes room so the frantic Bianca can cradle Cassio's head in her arms. He gets to his feet, glancing in disdain at Roderigo's body. "Gentlemen, I suspect this piece of trash was the one who injured Cassio." The lieutenant lets out a moan. "Rest easy, my friend," Iago offers, motioning to Lodovico. "My torch, sir." Lodovico hands it back to Iago, who holds the light over Roderigo. "Do either of you gentlemen recognize him?" They both shake their heads. Iago lowers his torch and bends for a closer look. "What on earth? – My friend and fellow Venetian, Roderigo! No, it can't be." He takes a second look. "But it is – my God, Roderigo!"

"What, from Venice?" Gratiano asks in disbelief.

"I'm afraid so, sir. Did you know him?"

"Know him?" Gratiano repeats warily, his voice sad, but uncomfortably so…

Iago notices this and widens his eyes in surprise. "Signior Gratiano? I beg your gracious pardon – forgive me if I forgot my manners and ignored you in all this commotion."

"I'm glad to see you," Gratiano says as he kneels by the body to see for himself.

Iago turns his attention back to Cassio. "How is it lieutenant?" He gazes into the pitch dark. "A stretcher!" he hollers at the top of his voice. "A stretcher someone!"

"Roderigo," Gratiano says quietly.

"He it is, yes," says Iago, nodding, when out of nowhere it seems, two brawny, rough-looking men in the attire of dockworkers appear carrying a stretcher and look to Iago.

"Finally, well done!" he tells them. "Be good men and take this fellow away, but carefully. I'll fetch the General's surgeon." The dockworkers set about placing Cassio on the stretcher, Iago forcing Bianca out of their way. "As for you, mistress, you can let him alone now." She watches in distress as the dockworkers hoist the stretcher and make ready to depart. Iago casts his gaze at Roderigo. "The man who lies dead here was a dear friend, Cassio. What was between you two?"

"Nothing," Cassio murmurs faintly. "I don't even know the man."

Lodovico, noticing that he's begun to shiver in the cold night air, takes off his coat and covers Cassio. Gratiano removes his as well and places it over Roderigo's blood-soaked body, adjusting it out of respect so his face is covered.

All watch grimly as the dockworkers bear Cassio off in the darkness.

Iago sneers at Bianca. "Why do you look so frightened? – Keep him warm, don't forget!" he shouts after the men carrying the stretcher, then sees Lodovico and Gratiano starting to move off. "Wait a moment, gentlemen." He turns to Bianca and grabs her by the chin. "I'll ask again: why are you so nervous, mistress? Can you see the fear in her eyes, gentlemen?" Bianca tries to free herself from his grip. "Don't look away like that," he warns her. "There'll be plenty of questions for you later. Take a look at our culprit, gentlemen, a good, close look. Do you see it? Yes, guilt always comes out, even when tongues are silent..."

"What has happened here?" Emilia demands from a short distance away. "Iago, what has happened?" she gasps in horror when she sees Roderigo's legs and feet sticking out from under Gratiano's coat.

"Cassio was attacked and nearly killed by this man and some others. They managed to escape but Roderigo here is dead for his pains."

"Unfortunate man," she says, staring at the wet blood all around. "Poor Cassio!"

"The result of whoring," Iago says with a mean look at Bianca. "Do a favor, Emilia. Find out from Cassio which woman he was seeing tonight." He notices Bianca is trembling. "Why are you shaking?" he asks.

"He was coming to see me," she says defiantly, " – but I'm not shaking because of that."

"Coming to you, was he? You will have to go with me then."

"Shame upon you, strumpet!" Emilia puts in.

"I'm no strumpet, but as honest a woman as you are," Bianca protests.

"As I am?" Emilia laughs. "There could be no chance of that..."

"Kind gentlemen," Iago says, addressing Lodovico and Gratiano who are eager to get going, "let's haste and see that poor Cassio's well looked after. Come mistress," he says to Bianca and grabs her by the wrist, "you will have a deal of explaining to do. Emilia, you run to the castle and tell my lord and lady what has happened."

Lodovico and Gratiano have the women precede them, while Iago lingers a moment beside Roderigo.

"I told you," he whispers, "this is the night that makes me, or ruins all and breaks me...."

The bedroom door creaks slightly in the darkness as Othello enters by the light of a candle he is carrying. He turns the key in the lock, quickly removes it and waits in silence, gazing over at the curtained four-poster bed where Desdemona is sound asleep, unaware of his presence in the room.

"I have just cause to do it," he says softly, "just cause, on my soul!" Moving across the room, he goes to the window and closes the drapes, pausing to gaze out at the night sky. "Don't have me explain it to you, you gentle stars – it is a matter of justice. And I'll not shed her blood nor scar that whiter than snow, smooth as porcelain skin of hers: yet she must die...before she betrays more men." The room darker now, Othello looks at his candle. "Put out the light – " he says to himself, forms his lips to blow, but at the last second lets out his breath away from the candle, his eyes falling on the sheer curtains around the bed to which he slowly makes his way. " – But then I have put out the light." He comes to a stop, shaking his head at the candle. "I extinguish you, flickering flame, and I can light you again if I choose to do so." By the side of the bed now, he gazes down at Desdemona. "But should I put out *your* light," he murmurs, "then, you shining specimen of excellent nature, I know not where, unlike Prometheus, I would find the fire to restore its light: once the rose is plucked I cannot make it grow again; it must wither." Parting the curtains, he leans close to her body, smelling her face and hair. "Oh balmy warm breath, that almost persuades the justice I feel to break its sword and flee!

"Once more it happens!" He stands up, his fists clenched in annoyance. "I weaken…" He pauses before bending down again. "Be just like this when you are dead," he whispers as though she can hear him, "and though I kill you, I will love you long after." He breathes in the smell of her skin once more, then kisses her. "Such sweetness was never so fatal to man… I would weep for you, but they would be cruel tears. This sorrow I feel is a strange burden, it hurts most where I love most. She wakes – " He steps back from the bed as Desdemona opens her eyes and sits up.

"Who's there? – Othello?"

"Yes, Desdemona."

"Are you coming to bed, my lord?"

"Have you said your prayers tonight?"

"Yes, my lord."

"If you thought of some sin for which you have not sought heavenly grace, seek it now."

"Please, my lord, what do you mean by that?"

"Only that you should do so and be quick. I will wait: I would not kill an unrepentant spirit. No, heaven forbid, I would not kill your soul."

"You talk of killing…"

"Yes, I do."

"Then, heaven have mercy on me."

"I pray that as well, with all my heart."

"I hope you are not talking of killing me…"

"Hum!" he moans.

"And yet I fear you, for you're cruel whenever you roll your eyes so. I don't know why I should feel afraid, since I know nothing about which I should feel guilty. And yet I do."

"Think about your sins."

"They are loves I bear for you!" she protests.

"And for that you must die," he says, and draws the curtains apart. She glares up at him. "That death's unnatural which kills for love." Othello turns his head.

"Alas, tell me why you are biting your lip? – Some vengeful passion shakes your very bones! These are signs. And yet I hope, how I hope they do not point to me – "

"Peace, be quiet," he tells her.

"I shall." With nervous hands she tucks her nightgown around her legs, sits a moment while silence hangs in the air. "So: what is the matter?" she asks.

His eyes shine in light from the candle. "That handkerchief which I so loved and gave to you, you gave to Cassio."

"No, by my life and soul, I did not. Send for the man and ask him."

"Sweet woman, take heed, take heed of perjuring yourself. You are on your death bed."

"I? – But not to die!"

"Yes, presently," he says. "Therefore you must confess your sins freely, for to deny the charges against you and swear they are false, cannot stifle nor persuade me away from what I have in mind to do. You are going to die."

Desdemona looks down at her hands. "Then the Lord have mercy upon me."

"Amen, I say."

"And 'Have mercy' you should too. I never wronged you in any way, never loved Cassio except as heaven approves with friends, I never gave him any token of my love, why would I?"

"I saw the handkerchief in his hands, by God! You lying woman," he says, fierce with anger, "you turn my heart to stone, you make me call what I intend to do murder, when I deem it no more than sacrifice for your crimes! I saw the handkerchief."

"He found it then," she fights back. "I never gave it to him. Have him brought here to tell you that himself."

"He has already confessed."

"Confessed?"

"That he has – God's death – been your intimate."

"Intimate? How?"

"He has."

"He will not say so."

"No, his mouth is closed now. Honest Iago has taken care of that."

"She heaves a sigh. "I fear the worst then. Is he dead?"

"Had all the hairs on his head been lives, my vengeance would have ripped out every one."

"Sadly," she says, her eyes brimming with tears, "he has been betrayed. And there is no hope left for me."

"Damn you, strumpet, will you weep for him in my face?"

"Banish me, my lord, but do not kill me." She reaches out and clutches at his coat.

"Down, strumpet!" He takes her by the arms and though she strains to hold on he shoves her roughly back on the bed.

"Kill me tomorrow, just let me live tonight!" she cries and wraps her arms around his neck.

"No, and if you fight – " He works to pull her arms away.

"But half an hour – "

"It is over with, there are no delays – "

"Let me say one prayer – "

"It is too late now – "

"Oh Lord! My lord – "

They grapple violently with one another on the edge of the bed, Desdemona holding her arms around him with all her strength until, in one quick movement, he bursts free, seizes her by the neck with one hand, while with the other he snatches a pillow and covers her head, leaning over her and pressing down with both hands and the full weight of his body. Her muffled cries go on for several minutes and then gradually weaken, as does the thrashing of her arms and legs. In a moment he relaxes his hands on the pillow and sits back, looking down at her lifeless body. Her nightgown has risen up almost to her waist in the struggle, so he pulls it down to cover her still, bare legs.

"My lord!" Emilia calls in a panicked voice outside the door and begins knocking. "What is going on, my lord? My lord, what is it?"

Othello casts his eyes toward the door where Emilia continues her urgent knocking. "What noise is this?" he asks, his gaze returning to Desdemona: there's movement under her nightgown. "Not dead? Not yet? I may be cruel but I am not unmerciful – I would not have you lingering in pain. So." He leans forward, pressing his hands on the pillow once more. "So."

" – Please, my lord? Open the door!"

"Who's there?"

"Let me have a word, my lord, I beg you!"

"Of course," he says, his voice not loud enough to be heard. "It's Emilia. Just a moment…" He glances at Desdemona. "Dead..." Emilia is knocking furiously now. Othello moves to sit on the edge of the bed. "She probably comes with news of Cassio's death." He turns again to Desdemona. "There was such noise…but no movement now… Still as the grave – "

"My lord!" Emilia cries.

Othello stares in the direction of the door. "Shall I let her come in?" he wonders. "Will it do me any good?" He turns swiftly. "I think she stirs again. No – what's best to do? If she comes in she'll want to speak to my wife." He's agitated at the thought. "My wife, my wife! What wife? I have no wife." He hunches over suddenly as if seized with a cramp. "Unendurable!" he wails, rocking his body back and forth. "Oh wretched moment! As if the eclipse of sun and moon has happened at once, and the terrified word gapes in awe at the change – "

"I beg you, my lord," Emilia cries in desperation. "Please let me speak with you! Please, my lord!"

"I had forgotten you," he murmurs and sits up on the bed. "Come in Emilia, but quietly." He gets up. "Just a moment." He draws the curtains closed around the bed and makes his way through the darkness. "Where are you?" he asks and the next moment stumbles against a footstool.

"My lord!"

"What's the matter?"

Reaching the door, he unlocks it and Emilia enters, extremely distressed.

"There's been a horrible murder, my good lord."

"What?" he asks absently. "A murder? When?"

"Just now, my lord."

"Probably the moon wandering off course," he says grimly, "coming closer to earth than she should, which drives men to madness – "

"No, my lord. It's Cassio. He killed a young Venetian named Roderigo."

"Roderigo killed, and Cassio too?"

"No, Cassio was hurt but not killed."

"Cassio not killed? Then murder is out of tune and the sweet music of revenge plays discordantly – "

"Falsely, he was! Falsely murdered!" Desdemona cries from her bed.

"Whose voice was that my lord?"

"That? What voice?" Othello pretends not to have heard and steps in front of Emilia so she can't see the bed.

"I know it – that was my lady's voice." Alarmed, she tries getting past Othello. He moves to block the way, but runs into a chair, which gives Emilia her opportunity. She dashes over to the bed and flings open the curtains, horrified by what she sees. "Help, help, oh goodness me, help!" she cries, shaking Desdemona's limp body. "O lady, speak to me! Sweet Desdemona, oh sweet mistress, speak to me!" Distraught, Emilia takes Desdemona's head in her hands and searches for signs of life.

"I died an innocent death," Desdemona says in a faint whisper.

"But who – who has done this, my lady?"

"No one. I myself." Her eyes flickering open slightly, she struggles to speak. "Farewell. Say goodbye to my kind lord…" Too weak to continue, her eyes fall shut, and a moment later she is dead.

Grief-stricken, Emilia can only shake her head and stare at the lifeless body before her on the bed.

"But, how could she have been murdered?" Othello demands coldly, coming over to stand by the bed.

"Alas, who knows?" Emilia mourns.

"You heard her say herself it wasn't I."

"She said so, yes," Emilia agrees and looks up, meeting Othello's eyes. "But I will have to tell the truth."

They look at each other in silence.

"Very well," he confesses, "she lied before going to burn in hell. It was I who killed her."

"Making her more the angel and you the blacker devil."

"She turned to sin, she was a whore."

"You demean her unjustly, you are the one who has sinned."

"She deceived and betrayed me."

"She did nothing of the sort – and heaven knows it."

"Nothing but copulate with Cassio!"

"Heaven knows she did not – "

"Ask your husband if you doubt me. You think I would risk eternal damnation by going to this extreme without every reason for doing so? Your husband knew it all."

"My husband?"

"Your husband."

"Knew that she was deceiving you? Out of wedlock?"

"Yes, with Cassio. Had she stayed faithful, heaven could have offered the most priceless gem in the world and I would not have given her up for it."

"My husband?" she asks, incredulous.

"He was the one who first told me. The most honest of men he is, and one who hates the slime that's spread by evil deeds."

"My husband!"

Exasperated, Othello glares angrily. "Why do you go on saying this? I told you: your husband."

Emilia gazes sadly at Desdemona. "Oh mistress, I fear some wickedness has made a mockery of your love." She casts her eyes defiantly at Othello. "My husband says she was unfaithful?"

"He, woman! I said your husband: do you not understand that word? My friend. Your husband. Honest, loyal Iago."

"If he told you that, may his pernicious self endure a long and painful death. It is a bold-faced lie! She was too caught up in her filthy black marriage to have done such a thing!"

"Haa!" Othello roars and raises his fist.

"Do what you must: this act of yours is just as unworthy of heaven as you were of her!"

"It's best you shut your mouth."

"You haven't half the power to harm me as I have to withstand the hurt you would inflict. You duped man, you fool, as dumb as dirt! You have done something – "

He draws his sword and, the same moment he thrusts it at her, Emilia grabs a pillow and holds it up so the weapon cuts through the cover, feathers flying as she hurls it at his face and slips off the bed, pulling the curtains with her which she flings in Othello's face as well. "Help!

Someone, help!" she screams and flees toward the door. "The Moor has murdered my mistress! Murdered her! Murdered her!!"

Rushing into the room with a detail of guards, Montano barely has time to get his hands up and catch Emilia as she runs into him. "What's the matter?" He looks to Othello by the bed, untangling himself from the bed curtains, his face and clothes covered in white feathers. "What is it, General?"

Staying by Montano, Emilia notices Iago, Gratiano, and the castle jester entering the room. "Oh, have you come too, Iago?" she says with sarcasm. "Haven't you done well that men are blaming you for the murders they do?"

"What is going on?" Gratiano demands, exchanging glances with Emilia, Iago and then Othello.

"Be a man," Emilia says to Iago, though her eyes are directed at Othello, "and prove this evil creature has lied. He says you told him his wife was unfaithful, yet I know you could not have, you are not the kind of man who would do something so vile. Tell these gentlemen and put my heart at ease."

Iago avoids her eyes. "I told the Moor what I thought, no more than what he found out for himself was likely to be true."

"But did you tell him his wife had been unfaithful?"

"I did," he says, glaring daggers at her.

"Then you told him a lie. A cruel, odious lie! A vicious, vicious lie, on my soul! Unfaithful with Cassio? Did you say with Cassio?"

"With Cassio!" he snaps at her, adding under his breath, "Mind your tongue, mistress."

"I will not mind my tongue, I must speak – " She looks at the others then points across the room. " – For my lady lies murdered there in her bed!"

"What?" cries Gratiano.

"How can this be?" Montano demands.

Emilia fixes her eyes on Othello. "He murdered her!" she rages, then turns on Iago, "and this man drove him to it."

"She's dead."

All look to Gratiano, who is by Desdemona's side.

"You need not stare, masters, it is indeed true," Othello says, grimly defiant.

"Horribly so…" Gratiano says gravely.

"Most vile deed," Montano frowns, aghast, and draws his sword.

"Horrible, horrible act!" Emilia shrieks. "I remember thinking so, I suspected it was so – " She throws Othello an accusing look. "I said it was a scheming soul at work, did I not? Let me die from grief!" she wails desperately and in a single move snatches Iago's dagger to stab herself.

"What are you doing – are you mad?" Wrestling his blade away from her, he shoves her to the floor.

"Wickedness!" she hisses at him.

"Go home, I tell you."

On her feet again, Emilia pleads with Montano. "Good sir, I beg you to let me finish. Until now my first obedience was to my husband – but it is no longer. Go home?" Her question to Iago hangs in the air. "Perhaps I will never go home, husband."

In torment, Othello collapses on the bed and strikes it with his fist. "No…" he moans, "No…"

"Go on then," Emilia says scornfully, "go on and howl, for you have killed the sweetest innocent who ever looked upon us."

"No, she was foul!" he objects, approaching Gratiano. "I hardly know you, sir, but believe me, your cousin who lies here, whose breath these hands indeed have newly stopped – I know it seems most hideous and cruel…"

Gratiano ignores Othello's protests. "Poor Desdemon, I am glad my uncle your father is dead. …This marriage was the death of him. Consuming sorrow broke his aged heart in two. Were he alive now, this sight would drive him to some desperate act – curse the angels watching over and ruin all he could."

"It is pitiful, I know," Othello explains, "but Iago will bear me out: she has committed the shameful act a thousand times with Cassio. He confessed to it, and she rewarded his amorous doings with the very token and proof of love that I had given her. I saw it in his hand, it was the handkerchief – the first token of his love my father gave my mother."

"Oh God!" Emilia gasps.

"Shut up, woman!" Iago threatens, still holding his dagger.

"It will come out, it will all come out! Shut up? No, I will speak as freely as the wind. Let angels and men and devils, let them all, all cry shame on me, but I will speak."

"Go home if you know what's good for you," Iago warns in a livid whisper.

"I won't."

Iago rushes forward, swiping his dagger fiercely at her throat, but Emilia pulls her head back just as Gratiano comes between them.

"Put up your blade!" he orders Iago.

With his sword out, Montano has the ensign do what he's been told.

Emilia turns to Othello as he comes off the bed, sword in hand, his eyes on Iago. "You stupid man," she says, "the handkerchief you speak of I found by chance and gave it to my husband because he had so often, with such serious determination – far more than such a trifle warrants – begged me to steal it."

"Degenerate whore!" Iago starts toward her but the point of Montano's sword stops him.

"Was it she who gave the handkerchief to Cassio?" Emilia asks, shaking her head. "No. I found it, and as I said, gave it to my husband."

"Harlot, you lie!"

"No, by heaven, I do not." She looks away from him to the other men in the room. "I do not gentlemen." She tries to catch Othello's eye but his stare remains fixed on Iago. "Oh you murderous fool," she says as if scolding and feeling sorry for him at the same time, "what was such a feeble man doing with a wife as good as she?"

Othello suddenly reacts, running at Iago with his sword. Montano brings his weapon forward, which allows Iago to duck swiftly behind a guard and bury his dagger blade in Emilia's back and chest several times before fleeing through the door and away.

Disarmed by Montano and his men, Othello watches Iago make his escape. "Is there no lightning heaven sends without thunder? Outrageous villain!"

Gratiano has the wounded Emilia in his arms but she's bleeding too badly for him to do anything. "The woman's collapsed, he's killed her."

"Yes, he has," Emilia labors to speak. "Lay me by my mistress' side…"

"He's killed his wife and fled," Gratiano says horrified, letting Emilia gently down to the floor, at which point Montano hands him the sword he has taken away from Othello.

"Use the General's sword and guard the door. If he tries to leave, kill him. I'll go after the worthless slave." He signals his men and they rush out in pursuit of Iago, Gratiano pulling the door closed behind them.

"I am not so valiant after all," Othello says to himself, "if they can get my sword from me so easily." He brushes stray feathers from his uniform. "How can reputation live on without that respect through which it was won?" He heaves a troubled sigh. "Be done with it…"

"What was your song's meaning, my lady?" Emilia's weakened voice makes itself heard in the stillness of the room. "Hark, can you hear me?" For a moment there is only silence. "I will play the swan and die to its music…"

Crouching down, Othello picks her up in his arms and carries her toward the bed. "*Willow, willow-willow,*" she sings softly, but stops suddenly and gazes up at Othello. " – Moor, she was always faithful…she loved you, cruel Moor, so goes my soul to heaven if I speak the truth! And speaking it…from my heart…alas…I die."

Othello lifts his gaze from Emilia's face, listening to the silence in the room for a moment. He goes around the bed and sets Emilia down beside Desdemona. He moves his lips, perhaps in a brief, silent prayer, but the next instant he is over at the closets, throwing the doors open and searching frantically through his personal effects: uniforms, clothes and regalia.

"There is another weapon here somewhere. My sword from Spanish days – with the blade tempered in icy mountain water." In a few moments he finds the handcrafted silver scabbard and draws out the sword: a truly magnificent, sharp and shining weapon. He comes back past the bed and goes to the door. "Cousin Gratiano," he calls, "I'm coming out."

"If you do, it will cost you dearly," Gratiano replies from the hall. "You have no weapon, after all. You wouldn't stand a chance."

"Come in and see me then, or, unarmed as I am, I'll go at you with my bare hands."

After a silence of several moments the door opens and Gratiano steps in, wary and cautious, his sword raised and ready.

"What is the matter?" He peers around the room looking for Othello when suddenly the General kicks the door shut behind him. Gratiano swings around only to feel the point of the Spanish sword against his throat.

"Do you see my weapon?" Petrified, Gratiano nods. "Better steel than this never graced a soldier's thigh, Gratiano…" Othello pulls the sword away and admires the blade.

"I have seen the day when, with this one arm and this good sword, I cut a path through twenty times the obstacles that could ever be put in a good soldier's way. But," he frowns in thought, "what good is vain boasting if, in the end, we can't control what is to be?"

Tensely brandishing his sword, Gratiano shakes his head.

"It's not that way with me now," Othello says. "Don't be afraid, though you see me holding such a weapon as this." He meets Gratiano's eyes, then glances around to take in the room. "This is where my journey ends, my final destination, the furthest point of all my voyaging…"

Gratiano is keeping his distance.

"There is no need to back away from me in fear, Gratiano. A man with little more than a bull-rush could charge at Othello now and he would turn and flee. But the question is, of course, where would he go?" He moves toward the bed and sits down next to Desdemona's body. "Now," he says, studying her face. "How do you look now? Poor, unfortunate girl, pale as the white cloth you wear. When we meet on Judgment Day this expression on your face will have me banished from heaven so that fiends from down below can snatch me away for their own." He places a hand on her forehead then touches her cheek. "Cold, cold my girl, just like your chastity. Oh cursed, cursed man! Whip me, you devils, until this blessed sight is driven from my mind. Blast me in the winds, roast me in the sulfurous pit, drown me deep in whirlpools of liquid fire!" He begins to cry. "Oh Desdemona, Desdemona. Dead – "

In a commotion of raised voices and fast-moving feet, Lodovico storms into the room with Montano, numerous officers, soldiers and the guard detail that has taken Iago prisoner. Cassio enters slowly behind them, his leg bandaged, guards on either side supporting him with arms under his shoulders.

"Where is this rash and most unlucky man?" Lodovico demands of Gratiano.

"Who once was known as Othello?" the General says quietly from the bed. "Here I am."

"The viper who preyed upon him," Lodovico barks. "Bring the man to me."

Two guards shove him roughly forward. A cold, indifferent look on his face, he stares elsewhere in the room.

"I look for devil's horns upon his head, but see none," Othello says. "It must be just a fable – " He gets up from the bed. " – But if you are the devil, then there is no danger this will kill you!" He springs at Iago and wounds him near the shoulder.

"Take his sword from him," Lodovico orders. Several guards do so, and pass the weapon to Lodovico.

"I may bleed, sir," Iago sneers at Othello, "but I am not killed."

"About that I am not sorry. I would rather you live, since it would be happiness to die."

"Oh Othello, who once was so admired," Lodovico says, looking with dismay at the blood-smeared sword. "What can we say, now that you practice treachery and evil too?"

"Why say anything, sir? I am an honorable murderer, if you will, for I did nothing out of hate but everything in the name of honor."

"This wretch has partly confessed to his crimes. He says you and he plotted Cassio's death together."

"Yes."

"Good General," Cassio protests, a hurt look on his face, "I never gave you cause."

"I understand that now, and I ask for your pardon. But I pray you, inquire of this less than human being why he so wanted to destroy me, body and soul."

"Ask me nothing. What you know, you know. From now on I will not say a word," Iago sneers sullenly.

"Not even to pray?" Lodovico asks.

"There are tortures that will open those lips of yours," Gratiano warns.

"Perhaps that is best," Othello says in answer to Iago's declaration of silence.

Lodovico motions one of his guards to hand over some documents. He turns to address Othello. "Sir, I can inform you of things that have happened but about which you may not know. Here are several letters found on the slain Roderigo, the first concerning the murder of Cassio, to be undertaken by him."

Othello glares at Iago. "Contemptible man."

"Most ruthless and most hateful," Gratiano adds.

"The other," says Lodovico, "is a litany of complaints which it seems Roderigo meant this villain to read, except it appears Iago talked to him before it was sent and gave some satisfaction in his answers."

"Loathsome coward," Othello says and glances at Cassio. "My wife's handkerchief, lieutenant. How did it come into your possession?"

"I found it in my room, but this vile man has admitted just now that he put it there himself, its disastrous effect the very thing he desired."

"Oh fool!" Othello says about himself. "Fool!"

"In one letter," Cassio carries on for Lodovico, "he also explains how it was Iago who forced him to challenge me while I was on watch, after which incident I was dismissed as lieutenant. Know as well, that just before he died, Roderigo told us how it was Iago who had tried to finish me off in the street when he had failed, and how it was Iago who then stabbed him and left him there for dead."

Lodovico shifts his gaze from Iago to Othello. "You are under arrest," he declares solemnly, "and so you must come with us, General. You are stripped of your rank and relieved of your command. Cassio will govern Cyprus in your stead. As for this worthless fellow, we will see every cruelty that torments him much and lasts for long, will be his. You will remain closely guarded in prison until news of what you've done is made known to the state." He turns to his guards. "Come, take him away."

Othello steps back as he's apprehended. "A moment, sir," he says to Lodovico, who is on his way out. "A word or two before you go."

Lodovico frowns, considering the request quickly, then nods for the guards to let Othello go so he can speak.

"I have done the state some service, and they know it: but let that be. I only ask that in your letters, when you write of my misfortune here, you speak of me as I am. Diminish not my guilt, but neither set my story down with malice to my name. Speak of me as one who loved not wisely, but too well; of one not easily made jealous, but who, when his worst fear was preyed upon, grew angry and afraid that what was precious had been lost, and thus, like lowly Judas, gave away the richest pearl of all; of one whose watering eyes, although unused to moods of tender-heart, shed tears as free as aloe shrubs their bitter healing drops. And say as well that in the pitch of battle in Aleppo, where one malignant, bruising Turk was set to kill a brave Venetian, I took him by the throat and thrust my dagger in his heart – like this!"

Moved by his words, the others are astonished to see him take out a knife he's had hidden in his jacket, and stab himself.

Lodovico cries, "Oh bloody end!"

"His words are now undone!" says Gratiano.

Still clutching the knife, Othello staggers as far as the bed and slumps down beside Desdemona. He steadies himself with a hand as he leans over her.

"I kissed you before I killed you. There is no way now, but this: killing myself, to die upon a kiss."

He puts his lips to hers, raises his head for a last look at her face and notices the hand folded over her chest. He lifts it up and sees that she is wearing his ring on her wedding finger, as well as her own. He closes his eyes and begins shaking his head, but only briefly. A short moment later, blood comes from his mouth. He rocks back and forth once and then falls from the side of the bed onto the floor, dead, Desdemona's lifeless hand hanging over the edge of the bed above him.

After a heavy silence, Cassio is the first to speak.

"I thought he had no weapon but feared this would happen, for he was always proud."

"You vile dog," a disdainful Lodovico says to Iago, "more vicious than hatred, hunger, or the sea. Look on the tragic burden with which you have loaded this bed: this is your work. The spectacle poisons sight, let it be covered up." Guards quickly pull blankets over the faces of the dead. "Gratiano, guard the house and seize the Moor's possessions, for they fall to you as Desdemona's nearest kin."

He turns to Cassio. "You, lord governor, will take charge of passing judgment on this villain as required by law, the time, the place, the penalty: be sure you do enforce it with all might. I myself will fast board ship, and to the state this heavy act, with heavy heart, relate…

New Directions

The Young and the Restless: *Change*
The Human Season: *Time and Nature*
Eyes Wide Shut: *Vision and Blindness*
Cosmos: *The Light and The Dark*
Nothing But: *The Truth in Shakespeare*
Relationscripts: *Characters as People*
Idol Gossip: *Rumours and Realities*
Wherefore?? *The Why in Shakespeare*
Upstage, Downstage: *The Play's the Thing*
Being There: *Exteriors and Interiors*
Dangerous Liaisons: *Love, Lust and Passion*
Iambic Rap: *Shakespeare's Words*
P.D.Q.: *Problems, Decisions, Quandaries*
Antic Dispositions: *Roles and Masks*
The View From Here: *Public vs. Private Parts*
3D: *Dreams, Destiny, Desires*
Mind Games: *The Social Seen*
Vox: *The Voice of Reason*

The Shakespeare Novels

Spring 2006

Hamlet
King Lear
Macbeth
Midsummer Night's Dream
Othello
Romeo and Juliet
Twelfth Night

Spring 2007

As You Like It
Measure for Measure
The Merchant of Venice
Much Ado About Nothing
The Taming of the Shrew
The Tempest

www.crebermonde.com

Shakespeare Graphic Novels

Fall 2006

Hamlet
Macbeth
Othello
Romeo and Juliet

www.shakespearegraphic.com

Paul Illidge is a novelist and screenwriter who taught high school English for many years. He is the creator of *Shakespeare Manga*, the plays in graphic novel format, and author of the forthcoming *Shakespeare and I*. He is currently working on *Shakespeare in America*, a feature-film documentary. Paul Illidge lives with his three children beside the Rouge River in eastern Toronto.